shared writing

Renga Days

writing

shared

Renga Days

writing

An anthology of nijuuin and hyakuin renga and
renga days on the renga platform, 2002–2004

Alec Finlay

platform projects
morning star
Yorkshire Sculpture Park
BALTIC Centre for Contemporary Art
ARTS UK

2005

Edition of 1,900 copies

Design by StudioLR and Alec Finlay
based on an original design concept by Colin Sackett

Published by:

platform projects
21a West Mayfield   www.platformprojects
Edinburgh EH9 1TQ   www.renga-platform.co.uk

morning star
Off Quay Building
Foundry Lane
Byker
Newcastle-upon-Tyne NE6 1LH   www.alecfinlay.com

Yorkshire Sculpture Park
West Bretton
Wakefield WF4 4LG   www.ysp.co.uk

BALTIC
Centre for Contemporary Art
South Shore Road
Gateshead NE8 3BA   www.balticmill.com

ARTS UK
Newburn Enterprise Centre
High Street
Newburn   www.arts-uk.com
Newcastle-upon-Tyne NE15 8LN   www.writingonthewall.uk.com

ISBN 0-9546831-4-5

contents

The renga platform in Lower Park, YSP; Alex Hodby and Gerry Loose facing.

via

Renga: a poem which effaces itself as it is written, a path which is wiped out and has no desire to lead anywhere. Nothing awaits us at its end: there is no end, anymore than there is a beginning: all is movement.
Octavio Paz

Shared Writing is a companion to *Verse Chain: Sharing Renga and Haiku*, a how-to guide for beginners. This second volume anthologises more *nijuuin* poems and illustrates the mushrooming of the renga platform project through residencies and tours around the British Isles. It also gives an account of our adventures in *hyakuin* renga, where poets compose one hundred verses over twenty-four hours.

The renga platform is like a stage and a temporary dwelling. For those who come to watch, the platform offers a quiet performance, for those who write it becomes a home. You don't need a platform to do renga and, using the schema, anyone can gather together a few friends and compose a poem.

Surely the project has taken root for sixty renga have been composed, some up mountains, others in woods or on the tube. The renga form has been adopted by Creative Writing MAs in Britain and America; Gavin Wade has composed a Socratic renga; Bill Herbert has made a *wronga*, inverting each image, turning a renga inside out; and Lesley Mountain has completed a solo renga. The renga platform has visited galleries, orchards and Roman forts and is now settled in Dharmavastu, a Buddhist retreat in Cumbria, where Subhadassi is running a renga season. Linda France is mastering a season at Langley. I have designed a permanent *woodland platform* for the hidden gardens in Glasgow, where Ken Cockburn is mastering a season. In my own private quarrel with time, I have recently embarked on a thousand verse *senku* renga, to be completed who knows when.

Renga will continue to grow and you can all be part of this because, of all poetic forms, this is the one that works for people who have never written before. *Shared Writing* features verses by established poets, expert haikuists and renga masters; but the bulk are by novices. Amateurism is no block, for renga offers a *via activa* and *via contemplativa*, a structure within which people can sit, listen and write, sharing in the decision-making. In this way renga goes beyond poetry: it is an art of communalism, or, if you prefer, a renga day is 'social sculpture', to adopt Joseph Beuys' terminology, and shared writing is a public artform.

Renga is oral and temporal before it becomes poem and print – the verses are so many notes for thoughts and feelings that pass between us over a day, as we share an experience of mood and strangers and friends connect.

The classical renga of ancient Japan recognised these poetic moods and codified them. A particular season or element took on a generalised meaning: autumn is sad; the full moon lonely. We in turn have naturalised these themes, which must be tweaked now and then to avoid cliché or japanoiserie.

The renga schema is a frame made of themes and this makes the poems a piece of contemporary anthropology. They portray a culture in love with interiors, warm chutney, malt whisky, moon worshipping, scrumping and walking. Sometimes it all seems a bit *Good Life*, but this is true to poetry's, especially haiku's, aspirational characteristics. Renga is our life as we'd like to think it could be. The photographs document a new craze, like an armchair version of Victorian Tweedy mountaineering, poets huddle on the platform writing sheets in hand.

When we began writing renga, the challenge was how to discover a native dictionary of season words, or *kigo*, equivalent to Japanese haiku. The answer was simple, do it by writing renga, for it is poems that shape a native tradition. The moon collage on pages 14–15 is an example of our breadth of imagery. Gerry Loose's love verse that suggested the Hebridean lonesome of someone away on an island became, through our teasing and enjoyment, a familiar theme at our renga days. As the isle was adopted for the theme of 'love' by other poets a native lexicon took shape.

The difficulty with schema is that they fix a path which may be at odds with the unfolding mood of a renga. Each day should preserve its own feel, as people settle together and a dynamic emerges. I wonder how many years it will take for the schema to be put aside?

During a renga day you may feel that you and the poem are out of kilter – you keep missing the mood. Feeling out of sorts, even dissenting, can release a verse intervention that is comic or parodic and undercuts the dominant tone. These verses are necessary, for they shake the poem up and shift it on, jettisoning a gentle mood that could, if it drifted for too long, sap the dynamic. Every few links the poem cries out for a simple utterance – *honey, we forgot/the dog; a carved cock/points west* – and we all laugh with a sense of relief.

In this book I have not credited the authors of individual verses. The poems are communal and they include many composite links that meld words or images by two or more poets. For me, the renga that succeed best are those which combine idiosyncratic and strong composite verses, for 'comp.' verses often 'turn' well, cutting together two images to shift scenes.

A link doesn't represent the peak of someone's creative possibilities as a soloist; rather it extends their ability to respond, to place a verse within a net of images where it belongs. Like comedy, it's all in the timing.

Renga is an art of listening and interpolation; a path that leads on and never ends.

Alec Finlay

sharing renga

- Anyone can take part in renga: three to twelve people gives the best dynamic (more limits discussion).

- Allow five hours for a *nijuuin* twenty-verse renga; fifteen minutes a verse, plus a break for lunch.

- Choose someone experienced to be a 'master' (or 'guide') and someone to be a 'host'. These roles can be exchanged during the day. The master and host lead discussion and choose verses, with the master having the final decision.

- Use the *nijuuin* schema for the season that you are writing in, or prepare your own schema.

- A schema is a thematic guide designed to prevent repetitions; but always be flexible and follow different moods.

- Take one page for your notes and verses; another to transcribe the selected renga.

- At each round everyone writes (in silence) then, if they wish, they offer a verse.

- Read the preceding (chosen) verse along with your own. The master selects one new verse, or suggests a composite verse combining elements of two or more verses.

- Listen to the different possible pairings until it becomes clear which one shifts or links in a generous way.

- A verse that is too clever can close a renga down; a quiet verse may be a good stepping stone.

- Strike out repetitions. In a renga something happens then it doesn't happen again.

- Everyone is listed as an author, regardless of whether they have a verse selected.

- The copyright of the poem is communal property.

- Take turns to make the tea.

(AF)

schema for nijuin renga   Martin Lucas

The opening verse (*hokku*) is a three line verse; the second verse (*daisan*)
is a two line verse. These templates are for guidance only, and variations
are expected.

		Spring	Autumn	Summer	Winter
Jo	1.	Spring	Autumn	Summer	Winter
	2.	Spring	Autumn	Summer	Winter
	3.	Spring *optional moon*	Autumn *opt. moon*	Summer *opt. moon*	Winter *moon*
	4.	No season	No season	No season	No season
Ha	5.	Summer	No season	Winter	Summer
	6.	Summer	Summer	Winter	Summer
	7.	No season	Summer	No season	No season
	8.	Love	No season	Love	Love
	9.	Love	No season	Love	Love
	10.	No season	Love	No season	No season
	11.	Autumn	Love	No season	No season
	12.	Autumn	No season	Autumn	Autumn
	13.	Autumn *moon*	No season *moon*	Autumn *moon*	Autumn *opt. moon*
	14.	No season	Winter	Autumn	Autumn
	15.	Winter	Winter	No season	No season
	16.	Winter	No season	No season	No season
Kyu	17.	No season	No season	No season	No season
	18.	Spring	Spring	Spring	Spring
	19.	Spring *flower*	Spring *flower*	Spring *flower*	Spring *flower*
	20.	Spring	Spring	Spring	Spring

the poet is an echo, even the moon is an artificial light

up early surprising the half moon in the river

lowering evening, half a thunder moon

face upturned to the silver moon, air fills and empties with the curlew's call

a mouse's shattered body, delineated by the moon

bruised lids, ocular light, a blue moon

new moon, the ice of her shut eye

an undertaker practices his tuba in the moonlight

his clarinet becomes the moon, becomes the river

my burning heart, cooled by the moon

night shift, moonlight catches falling sawdust

waiting in the half-light, suspended between moons

pull up the blinds and the moon will shine on buttered toast

mister, the game's a bogie, the moon's kicked intae the river

yer mammy's daddy says my daddy's a moon-man

subtle moon – gingerbread man in a circle

coat on back to front, hood full over, moonface waves me off

the last bus home – look at the moon, breath mists the window

caught without papers or pass, under a gallows moon

scattered thoughts, then the moon through the clouds

he breathes out it's only the moon

seeding honesty the waning moon reflected in his glasses

moon is not an option – every bloody night the same stupid mask

in the diary, ringed, Easter's full moon

14

first win of the season we follow the moon

Tyne Bridge softens, a pale pebble moon lies heavy on the water

emptying bookshelves the whole night – full moon

sun caresses the wood's blue carpet – would moon see colour like this?

out beyond the bay where the seals sported, moonlight on the sea

moon over the Pentlands, beech mast underfoot pops like seaweed

dew freezes, the outback radar is ranging the moon

on the mountains of the moon giant heathers, living obelisks

a wind from beyond the moon

another spaceship enters the orbit of the moon

the moon kissed by ripples, a broken teacup

rough cut oatcake moon

blue day warming, bees stir campion – whisp of moon

silken leaves circle in moon pools

cows sleep, leaves blow across the crescent moon

buckle-up! autumn moon, chill air

over stubble fields, the moon in the afternoon waxing towards winter

we paste down silver foil for a winter moon effect

dark night waits, moon slivers into the frozen pond

the garden around the moon, prickly with light frost

a hooded girl in moonlight, blue walks on the grass

a torrid night in the attic the moon slips through the panes

yesterday's moon still shining in the bowl of her throat

has the moon been watching? Its face is turned

The poem on the previous pages is a collage by Alec Finlay,
composed of moon verses written at *nijuuin* renga.

renga days, renga world

The renga platform has now been on tour for four years and its appearance is suitably bashed – the wood marked with dark teapot rings, grass stains and splinters; some planks are shot, and this is its third set of pins and screws. Note to Subhadassi: It could do with a good scrub and some danish.

The host venues have included Edinburgh's Scottish Poetry Library, Royal Botanic Gardens and Scottish National Portrait Gallery; SPACEX gallery in Exeter; a *matsuri* festival in West Calder; Scottish Natural Heritage's HQ at Battleby; Dundee Contemporary Arts; an orchard at the Swaledale Festival; and long stays in BALTIC and at Yorkshire Sculpture Park.

Other renga days have been held without the platform: in Lady Gregory's town house in Galway, during the *Cuirt*; in the deep purples of the Rothko Chapel, Houston, Texas; and a day of laughter in a tea house in Oloumouc (Czech Republic)

These three poems are a taste of the renga world. Others can be found on the website, www.renga-platform.co.uk

(AF)

candles by the river

a nijuuin renga in spring
Galway Arts Centre
13 March, 2004

Participants
Laura Brennan
Margaret Curran
Alec Finlay (master)
Mary O'Malley (host)
Tim Robinson
Gabriel Rosenstock (host)
Wendy Seviour

1 The bombings in Madrid took place
on 11 March, 2003; this verse records
the impromptu memorial candles lit
along the banks of the Corrib.

2 St Brigid's Eve is the first day of
Spring.

Below stone leaves
mould patterns grow
new blooms

    light floods in for a moment
    scented tea

mad
as March hares
the scudding clouds

    a white space held
    in the perfect skull

hot sun
yellow skirls from the beak
of a blackbird

    drowned in blaring horns
    streets quake

on a banner
at the foot of the screen
the death toll rises

    candles flame
    beside the river[1]

along the wall
cats stalk
one   another

    in the top window
    his hand rests on her shoulder

eyes absorb
watery light
evening yews

    the garden around the moon
    prickly with light frost

waves pound
the black rock –
a gull screeches on the shore

    my father stretches his limbs
    the floor sleeps under the carpet

drunken Sweeney
finds a bird
frozen to a stone

    blank page, blank stare
    snow all day

St Brigid's Eve[2]
a waking beetle
disturbs the earth's core

    the shrieks of children
    lengthen the day

hawthorn blossom
dots the pavement
snow again

    silent tender growth
    of the cell.

walking backwards

a nijuuin renga in spring
Swaledale Festival, Reeth
31 May, 2004

Participants
Anne-Marie Culhane
Alec Finlay (master)
Felicity Manning (host)
Amanda Ravetz
Tom Richardson
Shirley Ross
Beth Rowson (co-ordinator)
Elisabeth Sutherland
Tim Tunley
Stephen Watts
Frieda White

1 Set aside: land is in its 'natural state', which farmers are paid a subsidy not to farm so as to control overproduction.
2 During the Swaledale Festival the platform was sited in a renovated walled orchard in Reeth, also containing blossoming laburnum; the pods are poisonous.
3 A highlight of the Festival was a performance lecture by Jonathan Kenny, which included demonstrations on a number of rare and exotic instruments, including hollowed gourds from Central America and the carnyx, an ancient Scottish battle horn.
4 The meadows of Muker.
5 Stephen Watts, a friend of the festival, is well known for his penchant for walking backwards.

Yellow cups, oyster catchers
a fuss goes up
in the set aside[1]

    by a gate marked private
    she crouches among thistles

sharp in the reflecting pool
half a moon
fish slip into shadows

    still pulses
    the last blackbird

singing laburnum[2]
drop poison pods
where children play

    running in small circles
    with arms outstretched

kalashnikovs raised
bare feet
disturb the dust

    blown angels
    letters in a tin

vowels swim in linseed
shape and snap
on our tongue

    apple jelly smeared over peanut butter
    mother's one caress

flesh from the gourd –
the emptied shell
makes music[3]

    gives warmth, latitude
    the sun turns inward

under the bench
cracked water melon seeds –
night begins to bleed

    the soft order of quilts
    marshall my dream

in the nebulous
vapours form
a flake of snow

    wraiths will melt
    revealing fur and bone

knives and forks
on either side
of mismatched plates

    we catch our breath
    and turn over the earth

a million flowers
parted
by a path of stone[4]

    sure of the way
    the poet walks backwards.[5]

worst of all are the dwarves

a nijuuin renga in autumn
Čajovna Dřevěná panenká, Oloumouc
(Czech Republic)
12 September, 2004

Participants
Tereza Chocholová
Alec Finlay (master)
Robert Hysek
Martina Knápková
Jitka Svedirohová
Matthew Sweney (host)

1 a famous saying from 'Dlouhú, Široký
a Krátkozraký' by the legendary
playwright and inventor Jára Cimrman
(an imaginary character created by
Zdeněk Svěrák and Ladislav Smolják).
Mushroom hunting is a national sport
in the Czech Republic.

Do you mean mushrooms
she asked
or mushrooms?

    the forest
    echoes back

soft bubbling words
tickle stems
smatter caps

    river waters'
    winter colours

elephants
carrying
tea

    open blue doors
    for white clouds

close your mouth!
flies
rush in

    with their
    unplucked music

stretch your paws
air the bed
now it's time for love

    never mind the fleas
    your eyes bite

girls elsewhere
slower more
interesting

    the windows steamed
    to the very top

has the moon been watching?
its face
turned

    towards the wind
    come ravens

dress coats
and piercings
how bleak

    bulldozer breaking teeth
    trying to bury people

sharing honeycake
preparing
to shake hands

    it's time to squeeze pollen
    from the bees' asses

deer creep
seek salt
flowers are thirsty too

    worst of all are the dwarves
    you don't find them, they find you.

Writing in the Dark, Performance Space, BALTIC.
Photograph by Mireille Martel © 2003.

24

baltic renga

Two seasons of renga were hosted in various gallery spaces within BALTIC during my eighteen-month residency, most in my studio on Level 2 with its view over the Millennium and Tyne Bridges, which frequently found their way into the opening images of the renga.

For many people BALTIC was a phenomenon that glittered with promise and excitement, guarded over by Sune Nordgren, protestant visionary, utopian task master. It was also a place where thousands of visitors paraded through a building bereft of seats. The renga platform was one place where a few visitors could be still for a day, hidden away from monolithic exhibitions. The master and host poets at these BALTIC renga days included Ken Cockburn, Gerry Loose, Colin Will, Ira Lightman, John Cayley, W. N. Herbert, Linda France and Paul Conneally. These are some of the poems we made together.

(AF)

the family knot

a nijuuin renga in spring
BALTIC Centre for Contemporary Art,
Gateshead
8 March, 2003

Participants
Anne-Marie Culhane
Jorn Ebner
Alec Finlay (host)
Tessa Green
Morven Gregor
Bill Griffiths
Gerry Loose (master)
Tom Moody
Lesley Mountain
Jasmin Salter

1   *The Sky at Night*, long running
    television show on the stars, hosted by
    Patrick Moore.

The train south
geese flying north –
what else

    sun climbs slow
    stones pale and dry

the poet is an echo
even the moon
is an artificial light

    the wishing well
    filled with brown earth

tossing aside
a green penny –
digging up worms

    heat grinding skin flakes
    laughter from stroppy bushes

scolding the kids –
holding back
a smile

    the family knot
    is loose enough

I said
of course they will all
fit in the photo

    roots finger out
    from the frame

green tomato chutney
poured into
warm jars

    we shut the door
    while the radio plays

cosy together
watching
The Sky at Night

    4 am – the tide breathes
    through the house

across the bay
the hull
snow on fading paint

    waves burst
    cold shrapnel sweeps the pier

these mornings
the warship doesn't look
quite the same

    rolling up her trousers
    she wades through the river

a gleam
through overhanging branches
the first primrose

    we went home with handfuls –
    nothing more.

writing in the dark

a nijuuin renga in spring
BALTIC Centre for Contemporary Art,
Gateshead,
12 April, 2003
(in memory of Ric Caddel)

Participants
John Cayley (master)
Ken Cockburn
Jorn Ebner
Alec Finlay
Adam Fish
Tamsin Grainger
Ian Horn
Ira Lightman (host)
Marie Louise Lightman
Mireille Martel (co-ordinator)
Aidan Moesby
Annabel Newfield
James Johnson Perkins
Mathew Poole
Fiona Ritchie-Walker
Alistair Robson
Tracey Tofield
Graeme J. Walker

1 The pink pages, *Financial Times*.

Writing in the dark
we are with you – overboard
spring flowers at sea

    by the water invisible signs
    graffiti in bloom

salt on the window
a silver spoon rising
touches our lips

    the child asks
    over which shoulder?

toy boats are left unsupervised
these are the rules – no chucking,
in the nettles is out

    and no picking –
    they're not ripe yet

cumulus close
fuzzy boundaries – shut your eyes
count to a hundred

    but slowly
    slowly

what of this is yours?
mine? I have counted every
rain drop on your face

    September caesura –
    sudden changes send us crashing

in the pink pages
flaring empires
bull markets

    fall: of the blankets bombing
    the cool beds we have to make

there is a limited radius
we can walk within –
sanctioned light bulb

    emotions are given capital –
    you can see perfectly well

mirrored arrows
land softly on you –
a crystal blizzard

    crack! from here to there
    measured in a stone's throw

whatever it was
no regrets – and I seem . . .
to . . . have forgotten the rest

    I've had a skinful
    of songs' first lines

in the wreck
voices
wreathed in anemones

    taste
    the perfumed water.

rent web

a nijuuin renga in summer
BALTIC Centre for Contemporary Art,
Gateshead,
9 August, 2003

Participants
Ira Lightman (master)
Alec Finlay (host)
David Alton
Kathy Atkinson
Mary Atkinson
Trevelyan Beyer
Andy Hodson
Ness Kennedy
Irene Leake
Linda Martin
Matthew Poole
Florence Ridley
Mike Smith
Tracey Tofield
Tamatha Weisser

I swim in summer
up to the neck in icy blue –
lazy cats watch us

    hills a hazy distance
    hear the seagulls cry

Tyne Bridge softens –
single pale pebble
moon heavy on the water

    slipping into sleep
    dreams of other lives

how to choose
long straws, short straws, a breeze?
hey, you there –

    leaves disintegrate underfoot
    wood smoke my perfume

veiled sodium lamp
empty car park, a rent web,
the window shut at night now

    flung pan clang into metal sink –
    a bell in the calm

words have no meaning –
is sorry so hard to say?
perhaps not

    love coughs a seed
    a plum stone in the throat

gush of wild
honey – wild gush
of the tongue

    dinner on our knees –
    a dismembered torso on the tele

after
you unravel the sheet
scour until the liquid runs clear

    haunt the hill tops
    freezing sunsets are best

worsted mitts,
pictured on cognac
'The Retreat from Moscow'

    you crawl
    out of the souterrain

there's no maths to it
to know how far clouds are –
all day people fly

    into the light
    colours go everywhere

Iris waves
yellow flags
for Cornucopia's National Day

    a butterfly waits
    and should it stay?

from sea to sea

Writing on the Wall is a calendar of events that Steve Chettle of ARTS UK programmes along Hadrian's Wall and he invited me to tour the platform from sea to sea. In September 2003, and again in 2004, we packed the plattie up in a red Brambles hire van and made our way along that winding stone line.

The eight renga took place roughly every ten miles, each one sketching a poetic map of what we could see, weaving in a little of what we learnt along the way. We lolled on cushions in a commander's villa, set up in historic camps, mile forts, a school, even the dusty back room of the church at Heavenfield. It was hard work as we ran the renga day-on, day-off, shifting the plattie into some tight spaces along the way. There is a satisfaction in getting to know your turf and marking off the points on such a journey.

Morven Gregor came down from Glasgow for every renga day and took a gallery of photographs, as well as chipping in some finely chiselled links. Irene Leake became our renga follower in 2005, staying at B&Bs and hostels and travelling by The Wall's own tour bus. Penny's boyfriend treated her to a renga for her birthday and she travelled all the way from London to Dharmavastu. That first year Ken Cockburn and I did our debut school renga, with Sheree Mack and pupils at Walbottle.

This is our chart of The Wall.

(AF)

arbeia renga

I'd begun to regard the reconstructed Commander's House at Arbeia as almost a personal, intimate space, ever since I'd taken a class from Hadrian Primary in, just as it was being completed. We were the first people to visit and I was struck by the fact that the school occupied the same site as the *vicus*, that is, the civilian settlement which sprung up outside any Roman fort.

When one of the archaeologists let us into the room where he was sorting out the different finds, and we started making notes about the bones and potsherds he'd just uncovered, it felt like we were having the same experience as those first visitors to the original camp might have had, only we were looking back from the twenty-first century, like looking down the wrong end of a telescope.

So when I walked in on Alec Finlay brewing up some green tea in a little Japanese iron pot, his kettle attached to a highly anomalous-looking plug in the wall of the summer dining room, it felt as though that domestic space had undergone a subtle wrench. Suddenly here we all were, sitting on the big couches the Roman officers and their families would have eaten from, sipping a beverage unknown to them and contemplating a poetic form unknown to most Westerners until relatively recently. The room was cold yet bright, high-roofed with little mullioned windows, evidently designed for another climate. It was as though we were at once entering the past and unable to live in it.

We had to find a way of aligning all these very present layers with the sinuous length of the *nijuuin* renga, its seasonal slippages and subtle allusions to the human heart. Was our starting season, for instance, still (just) summer or incipient autumn? I've been struck by the way the references to the seasons in renga throw you on the resource of memory as a source of inspiration, yet the actions of spontaneous composition and continual reading aloud constantly returns you to the present moment.

The cultural leap we all attempt in writing this most particular of foreign forms seemed at once compounded and encapsulated by the further layers of history around us, and the strange status of this rebuilt half of an ancient house, with its own speculative reconstructions made concrete just as our own memories and cultural assumptions were being translated into the developing chain.

An unexpected burst of sunshine meant we lingered rather long over an al fresco lunch, watching the huge funnels of a cruise ship sliding past the end of the fort and between the houses that face the river. I'd been thinking all day about L. S. Lowry, his fascination with the boats that enter the Tyne between the two great breakwaters, and again it seemed to me that the grain barges and supply ships of the later empire must have seemed as large and inexplicable to any local sitting here seventeen hundred years ago. Miles Thurlow actually fell asleep briefly in the exact pose Lowry used for the man lying on a wall smoking – and echoed in the long torso of an oil tanker, with the smoke stack punning on the cigarette.

We had to hurry to catch ourselves up and get back into the steady rhythm of creation – and Steve Chettle's haiku about the Vindolanda texts enabled me to drop the only lines of Latin poetry found so far on the Wall into the mix: a single phrase from Virgil given as a handwriting lesson to a child. Somehow it fitted.

W. N. Herbert

dove white

a nijuuin renga in summer
Arbeia, South Shields, Hadrian's Wall
3 September, 2003

Participants
Steve Chettle
Alec Finlay (host)
Margaret Frayne
Morven Gregor
W. N. Herbert (master)
Miles Thurlow

1 L. S. Lowry, the artist.
2 Recreations of Roman wall paintings depicting fruit trees and birds decorate the Roman Villa at Arbeia.
3 *Soon hasty fame thro' the sad city bears / [The mournful message to the mother's ears.]*; Dryden's translation.

That gull could be a cloud,
Lowry , a legionary:
its wing refuses

    over the sea the sky tilts
    light falls slanting away

clear morning –
a slug draws slow
silver excretions on warming stone

    dove white emulsion
    protects from damp

its old roof removed
the fort is filling up with
air's blue granaries

    painted pears wait[2]
    for the afternoon sun

impatient hands –
conkers take their time
to fall

    cargoes of people wave
    sailing between the houses

at the corner shop:
The Chronicle, sausage rolls,
endangered fish

    a post box swallows
    the taste of the stamps

thin veneer scripts –
birthday guests
a line of Virgil

    interea pavidam volitans
    pinnata per urbem[3]

night's errata:
for shooting stars
read satellites

    the little panes make ice cubes
    out of the low sunless sky

fake snow
lying in drifts
deep into February

    sorry, I fell asleep –
    my toes seem larger now

hurrying to school
the mothers don't notice me
get out of their way

    parked outside the Mithraic Temple
    a pram wheel chariot

hungry now
the kids' egg sandwich:
anemone and celandine

    making do
    is the best of beauty.

walbottle technology college renga

I have run poetry sessions in schools for several years, and participated in and mastered renga platform events before, but this was my first renga with school pupils. I was curious, perhaps even apprehensive, as to how it would go. I travelled from Edinburgh to Newcastle on the 7.35 a.m. train. It was a fine late summer morning, and a joy to watch the fields and the woods pass by, before the lines began to run next to the sea.

When I arrived at the school the platform was being set up beneath a tree on a corner of grass near the main entrance. I joined the others slotting the lengths of wood together. A small wild garden, with an overgrown pond, lay immediately behind; then the school on two sides, but far enough away not to be intrusive; in front, beyond the drive, was an expanse of playing fields. The school boundary was formed by the remains of Hadrian's Wall, now just a dip in the ground, and a row of trees. We were on the barbarian side; the Romans would have been stationed where the main road now runs.

Interestingly, I also heard that much of the wall was only dismantled in 1745-46, after Bonnie Prince Charlie had marched south through Cumbria, and the Hanoverian commanders realised that they couldn't transport their serious weaponry east to west to counter this. The wall provided accessible road-building materials.

The location worked perfectly. The platform felt a part of the life of the school, but removed enough from it to let us work as we wished; and seemed to be an extension both of the school buildings and of the open space around them. Because of the school timetable we had less time than usual to write, just over five hours as opposed to the six or seven usually needed to write a twenty-verse renga. I didn't know how quickly the pupils would grasp the renga concept, and anticipated writing maybe sixteen verses, thinking in the back of my mind that even this might be pushing it. The weather stayed fine and the pupils arrived, not reluctantly but with some uncertainty. I gave a little talk about the renga 'rules', then after I'd provided a first verse and Alec a second, we were off. They quickly got the hang of it. What was unusual about this event was the amount of editing and combining of offered verses which Alec and I did as we went along – verses which had an arresting image or phrase, but didn't quite work overall. Four verses of the renga are 'combinations' and others were revised following discussions among the group. As usual on the platform, the time passed easily, with neither a sense of pressure nor of time dragging. The mix of adults and teenagers seemed to work, though I think by the end the pupils were all very tired, as I had been the first few times I sat on the platform. The amount of mental energy one can expend is surprising. Over time I've developed an awareness that the easiest and most fruitful way to write is to open oneself to thoughts and sense experiences, and then to describe and annotate these, rather than willing poems into being. But it takes practice. In the end we completed an eighteen-verse renga, deviating from the schema by cutting the 'No Season' verses 4, 8 and 9, then adding a final 'No Season' couplet when we realised that otherwise we would finish on a three-line verse. Eight verses were by adults, ten by teenagers, which is only slightly out of proportion to the numbers of each sitting on the platform, six and nine respectively. Rereading the renga now, if anything strikes me it's a certain impersonal-ness or abstraction about the language, especially through the middle section. Not an 'I', 'we' or 'you' to be found, and even the 'me' of 'forget-me-not' refers to a flower as well as the speaker. The 'love verses' (7 and 8) feature 'coldness' and snogging rather than anything more tender or touching. And there is less humour than one might expect. But the concrete images stand out well in such a setting — 'twisted sheets', 'horse teeth', 'bald orange head', the heartbeat. Certainly it has encouraged me to believe that the renga platform is a project which can work in a school setting.

Ken Cockburn

hadrian's ghost

an eighteen-verse renga in summer
Walbottle Campus, Hadrian's Wall
5 September, 2003

Participants
Jane Allen (Y11)
Jon Aydon (Y11)
Rebecca Boyd (Y13)
Lauren Bromley (Y11)
Ken Cockburn (master)
Leanne Conway (Y13)
Alec Finlay (host)
Morven Gregor
Kate Henderson (Y13)
Laura Hollocks (Y11)
Sheree Mack
Laura Steventon (Y11)
Miles Thurlow
Louise Wallbanks (Y11)
Hayley Wright (Y11)

Rosebay willow-herb –
summer's pink is loosening
to weightless white down

    spider lines muss the folds
    of your floppy sun hat

light cascades –
star circles rest
in the warm night

    twisted sheets
    at dawn

cold sweat –
leaves through the bars
carpet the concrete

    surge through stripped trees
    sink into mush

deception, deceit –
his devotion to coldness
deep as a ditch

    horse teeth, long tongue
    beauty of the bike shed

gleaming might
commands the river –
scenery slips by

    fixed to the wall
    a bald orange head

Hadrian's ghost
walks the line
protecting stones

    squares of light
    seep through the fog

compacted air
choking the dancers –
the beats throb

    is it his heart drumming
    through the church?

Easter
falls so late it bumps into
Mayday, the pagan

    forget-me-not
    forget-me-not

a year of dust –
the chintz endures
another spring clean

    the old woman
    drinks her tea.

Housesteads.

housesteads renga

We are seated on a fine-crafted wooden platform under a bright sky with
fast moving clouds. There is a clear view of small hills and valleys to the
south. To the north, at our backs, are the foundation stones and footings of
a fort. Behind that is a wall running from coast to coast, east to west across
the north of a small country. Built as a barrier to deter the people from
another, smaller country, further north, from cross-border raids and as a
statement and consolidation of empire, it's now in disrepair, with whole
stretches in ruins.

We are here to make a collective poem. We have come from all
quarters, both sides of the wall and further afield, gathering, like the
garrisoned troops before us with common purpose. Our purpose is the
antithesis of theirs. They held (and were held) by force of arms. All poems
speak for life; recognise no boundaries.

Those troops, from Algeria, Turkey, Syria, Gaul, Morocco, at the edge
of empire, look over our shoulders, jostle our elbows as we write. As we
breathe clear air they exhale. We remember their dreams for them. We
scrutinise their stonework. We make close observations of the local plants
and safely grazing sheep who never glance up at the lit clouds. We spend
the entire day in their company, breaking bread with them, sharing our
hot drinks, fleshing the poem.

By the day's end, packing the platform, we've come to a surer
knowledge of that hilly landscape in its sweep and its particularity of tiny
herbs. We've located commonality with the soldiers: their dreams become
ours; our spans the same. The land and its poem remain memories of
laughter in summer and cloud shadows, as if in time-lapse photography.
In the funnel of days our poem states, simply, we were here.

Gerry Loose

roman holiday

a nijuuin renga in summer
Housesteads, Hadrian's Wall
7 September, 2003

Participants

Alec Finlay (host)
Morven Gregor
Margaret Hall
Irene Leake
Gerry Loose (master)
Sadie Pape
Pauline Plummer
Ruth Sheldon
Miles Thurlow
Louise Wellington
Ezekiel Williams

1 A complete Roman latrine at
Housesteads.

Mint at the wall base –
all that's left
of legions' dreams

    the cat stretches
    in the middle of the path

patting a butterball
across
the afternoon sky

    moss blurs green
    angles of walls

bare fields
patterns of facts –
trigonometry

    spiders shelter
    trees begin to blaze

set the kindling
your way –
let's eat

    hot soup in bowls,
    grandma talks and talks

a blaring sound
in the distance
the morgue gets another

    from her to him
    just a glance

buckets of laughter
echo
from the latrines

    bacon and sausage
    tea bags and legs

this one's tagged
FINAL DEMAND
for this quarter

    a shiver –
    all accounts are empty

paper and ribbon
tangle
in the pine

    no kite ever unscram-
    bled its own lines

spare change chinks
in the bottle –
who will I holiday with this year?

    waking is easier
    in the earlier dawns

the blossom on that tree
been there for ages –
where am I?

    we walk further
    gather nettles and sorrel.

Heavenfield Church.

heavenfield renga

At Heavenfield it's hard to tell if it's you that's high or the sky that's low. As soon as you step off the Military Road and walk through the gate next to the sturdy wooden cross, you're in meadow – buttercups, grasses, dock – and the clouds roll over your head east towards the city and the sea.

The old stone wall round the churchyard borders sycamore trees and nettles, lush and rampant green above and below. A blue swing sways in the breeze: you watch it and the way your thoughts weave in and out of everything that's there and everything that isn't; the sounds of birds and sheep and cars in the distance. You can smell animal and earth, a hint of autumn in the air – ripeness.

In the graveyard you can sit on a seat of wood and stone and see the whole of the North unfold in front of you, the blaze of the Cheviot on the horizon. A metal plaque tells you it's dedicated to one Alexander Mason, born at Heavenfield on 2 June, 1906 and died a couple of miles along the Wall at High Brunton on 6 February, 1997. That seems to suit this place, so deeply rooted in time and continuity, where what is important can bear fruit.

Rain will thread you into the church, the small fusty vestry, cluttered with heaters and hymn numbers, boards telling you the story of King Oswald and how a heavenly light appeared all night over his bones and invested them with the power to deliver souls possessed with devils. And so your thoughts find new hooks to hang themselves on, a different quality of light to see by. Working with renga, it occurs to you, it's not by hand you write but by breath, coming and going, open as the sky over Heavenfield.

Linda France

cloth wings

a nijuuin renga in summer
Heavenfield, Hadrian's Wall
9 September, 2003

Participants
Steve Chettle
Alec Finlay (host)
Linda France (master)
Margaret Frayne
Morven Gregor
Irene Leake
Sylvia Lynch
Aileen McKay
Lesley Mountain
Sadie Pape
Anne Race
Jadzia Race
Eileen Ridley
Miles Thurlow

1 Heavenfield: site of battle between
Oswald of Northumbria and
Cadwalla of Gwynedd in AD 635.
2 The Saint's bones were ascribed
miraculous powers of healing and
led to a cult of St Oswald spreading
throughout Europe during the
Middle Ages.

Another blue sky
shaking itself free
of swifts

    leaf shades
    on bamboo

a wind
from beyond
the moon

    secrets pass
    between the yew trees

branches crack underfoot
a phone rings –
where are my shoes?

    if it's a bear play dead
    for a lion fight back

she wakes
to tawny light
spilled on her pillow

    a blanket laid over
    the field of battle

Vs in the mud –
the wall's not Roman
anymore

    at the edge of the forest
    a vixen seeks a mate

the stirrup cup
lathered flanks,
saddle sore

    soap bubbles squeeze
    from the sponge in your hand

butterfly cakes
bowl licked clean –
happy kids

    cloth wings hang
    in the cupboard

scratching a spy hole
on the frozen pane
I see a fire

    why do you keep on
    telling me fairy tales?

St Oswald's bones,
a candle burning
through the afternoon

    sunlight bends and flexes
    a hare's hind legs

purple shadows
yellow coltsfoot
could shift tarmac

    kestrel silhouette
    moves away.

my first renga

Around half past nine I walked downstairs into the light of an (early) autumn morning. The night's rain had gone. I was full of anticipation.

I'd been looking forward to a day of renga ever since Linda France had first talked so enthusiastically to me about them some years before.

Everything came in a red van – an iron tea pot which was put to work almost immediately; big bare beams and slats made of Douglas fir; meditation cushions and mats; Beth and Alec with their hats.

Within an hour, after some malletting and drinking of green tea, the pick'n'mix of objects from the back of the van had been beautifully organised in space, and we were ready to start.

I loved having the excuse to sit all day in my own garden, beside the old crooked apple tree weighed down with Bramleys, in sight of a living Douglas fir that towers over the whole of Sandysike. It was great to see this place I've become inured to over the last couple of years through others' eyes.

This borderland with Hadrian's Wall speeding through it like an arrow, its presence (visible or invisible) trailing long and low.

I enjoyed the communal making of the poem. What, as a writer, I usually do in the privacy of my own head, or at the privacy of my desk, I did with others, out in the open. We all shared our newly-minted lines and phrases without having had time to worry about their quality. This process was a great antidote to preciousness, and self-obsession. Who owns the poem? We all do. Very liberating.

And there was more. There I was, both a Buddhist trying to practise Buddhism in a Western context, and a poet trying to bring the spirit of Buddhism (honesty, clarity, sensitivity, appreciation) to bear in his life, in his work. And I was engaging in an ancient Japanese art form, which embodied so much of the simple formal beauty of Buddhist practice with other Westerners in the grounds of a new rural Buddhist Retreat that I'd been involved in setting-up.

So, as well as the *fact* of it, it meant a lot to me symbolically. That conversation between the best of the east and the best of the west. The coming-together of something of western and eastern literary and artistic traditions. And because it was practical, because *we did something rather than just talked about it*, the day went under all the potential froth and blather of such ideas into our lived experience.

It was good.

Subhadassi

talking on the lawn

a nijuuin renga in autumn
Dharmavastu, Sandysike, Hadrian's Wall
6 September, 2004

Participants
Steve Chettle
Penny Dunbabin
Alec Finlay (master)
Morven Gregor
Irene Leake
Sara Lurati
Beth Rowson (co-ordinator)
Subhadassi (host)

1 Sandysike is surrounded by high chestnuts; old apple trees grow in the garden.
2 A stone circle near Penrith, Cumbria.
3 The watermill at Little Salkeld, down the road from Long Meg.
4 Seasonal Affective Disorder.

Alone with that old conker[1]
the one thing you'd miss
is an enemy

    cut stone laid heavy and high
    sour Bramleys, garden moons

breathe in damp air
listen to the silence
on the derelict frontier

    a cloud shrouded growl,
    what is its range?

turning left on the plane
lipstick smiles
greet each passenger

    he took his Powerbook everywhere
    even Halkidiki

a wall of heat
bleached umbrellas
jig on the sand

    gingerbread curls
    peel on the barge

a pebble skims
across
a superstition

    brush my hair at midnight
    waiting for a face

crossed fingers touch
an admiral
in the mirror

    knick of the blade
    tissue paper dab

bodily fluids, longings,
candle nub ends,
they recycle all they can

    snow angels
    on the lawn

for 4,000 years
Long Meg and Her Daughters[2]
haven't felt the cold

    the mill doors[3]
    open wide

smell of bread
pumped through
every supermarket

    the clocks go forward
    an end to S.A.D.[4]

billowing above the drive
gentians
on a linen pillowcase

    we've been talking all day
    on this hard bed.

kirkandrews-on-eden

It's a clear, bright morning when I arrive in Kirkandrews-on-Eden, a small settlement north-west of Carlisle. I find the renga platform set up beside the village hall, looking down across the river Eden and the baled fields. Alec Finlay, Beth Rowson and Morven Gregor are tootling around, picking brambles and chatting – Morven telling how she'd walked close enough to spit on the monument to King Edward I, 'The Hammer of the Scots', planted on Burgh marsh where he died of fever in 1307.

I was born in Bowness-on-Solway and grew up in Burgh-by-Sands, just up the road. This is part of the reason I've been invited to take part in the renga. But I've never done one before and I'm a little nervous. I'm not sure before we start that I will be able to contribute appropriate verses. I have performance anxiety. I'm the 'host' for today and Alec, as 'master', will ask for my opinion at certain points; I worry that I won't have an opinion and that my reputation as a 'local' – and a 'poet' – will soon be rung hollow from the open-sided, wooden platform.

The group gathers and we begin by deciding which season it is that we're working in, as this decides in what order the verses of the renga are put together. Autumn, it's decided. I'm pleased, because a week ago I felt a draught blowing in from the end of the year, a very recognisable chill as the summer gave way. So I'm beginning to feel more at ease: we all agree where we are. And a sense of this agedness, along with the ripe immediacy of brambles, begins our poem.

A renga, it turns out, is a strange mixture of the personal and the communal, of the here-and-now and the recollected. As the day goes on, and the blinds are let down to block the sun, we all offer verse after verse, and by continual reading-out decide which verses or lines should be added to the poem, which gradually becomes a record of the day itself and an infusion, prepared as each member of the group allows their own particular perceptions and tone to be considered. It's the renga master's job to take responsibility for the shape of the poem, which is really a responsibility to the shifts of scene and season that occur between each obliquely-linked verse; and to how much potential a presented verse has as a jumping-off point for the next: the renga, like any poem, is propelled onwards, as it is being composed, by how much what has just been said reveals what has yet to be said.

Perhaps, in pontificating about the process, I'm hiding more than I'm revealing to you. The six hours are utterly simple: a twenty-verse renga is composed, verse-by-verse, by a mixture of consensus and Alec Finlay's firm guidance. For the whole day I feel a strange peacefulness. There are moments when I imagine I can spend the rest of my life around the platform, watching, recording and recalling the seasons and experiences I've already had. For me the renga on this particular day, and maybe any day, is full of voracious melancholy: there is so much to look at and to smell, and so much that has been touched and tasted that we long to touch and taste again.

Jacob Polley

the river runs backwards

a nijuuin renga in autumn
Kirkandrews-on-Eden, Hadrian's Wall
8 September, 2004

Participants
Margaret Boumphrey
Steve Chettle
Alec Finlay (master)
Morven Gregor
Alan Hodgson
Stella Hodgson
Irene Leake
Sara Lurati
Jacob Polley (host)
Beth Rowson (co-ordinator)

1 Chapelcross, the four towers of the nuclear power station visible over the Solway Firth.
2 The garrison along the wall included conscripts from Morocco.

Nettles and old docks
with liver spots,
inky brambles

    seedy teeth
    cobwebs muss my lips

Screech owl
cuts through
night's comfort

    barely awake
    but the sun says *make, make, make*

Chapelcross at full blast –
the black melting road and wood
the light's broken into

    chalked silhouettes
    a flick of the line

tamped
the best Havana
scented air rolls out

    rum, lime and mint
    faded mojito bars

remember the hay barn?
I pulled the gold straws
from your hair

    in that pause
    she becomes another

glimpse of blue
her quick eyes
the river runs backwards

    a pair of herons
    angled dance

look
what the waterfall's
done to the moon

    jabbing at the crazed glaze
    the stamp surfaces

where is it from?
the magi follow
a black smudged star

    on the wall
    a Berber guards snow[2]

marked on the OS
every bridge
every pylon

    at Alballava's an orchard
    sheltered by ash

Judas ears
and ramsons sushi,
the perfect picnic

    tupperware lids
    not quite fitting.

wall's end

The renga was held in the garden of the Wall's End Guest House. I arrived early, drove straight past (accidentally) and ended up going all the way through the village of Bowness until I had a view of the marshes and the Firth stretching beyond. It turned out to be a useful detour, because the view surfaces at verses 4 and 20 in the renga, and it helped to have seen it first hand.

The garden wasn't obviously an ancient historical landmark, but if you built a wall, however imposing, you wouldn't expect one end of it to still be visible 2000 years hence. For me, the renga wasn't about history, Roman or Japanese, it was about Now. This meant following the shifting moods of the weather and the rises and falls of the creative energy of the group. We built the platform on a lawn among the trees, in the place most likely to catch the sun. At first it seemed we had miscalculated, but by late morning the sun had wheeled round to reach us, and the spirits of the group were high. In early afternoon the day cooled, and a breeze got up, scattering leaves and rustling our papers. The liveliness of the weather seems to be reflected in the wild leaps of the central section of the poem, as it visits Valletta and the Mountains of the Moon. Then the wind dropped, and the day grew quite dark, and still and humid. Mosquitoes gathered, and the great outdoors lost a little of its charm. I threw in a link that landed us on planet Mars, buried in a crater, out of all radio contact with Earth. Somehow we found our way back to where we'd started, somewhere at the end of the wall down by the Solway Firth.

Many of the liveliest links in the renga were contributed by participants with little or no experience of the form but who soon got the hang of it. But what does getting-the-hang-of-it mean, as far as renga writing is concerned? It means you follow where your mind goes. If a lizard's tail prompts the image of a curling bookmark, don't reject it as an irrelevance. If the sound of cracking ice transforms into the sound of a crackling fire, allow it, accept it. When you embark on a renga you have no idea where you're going and there are several voices offering directions. But that's just it: an imaginative journey; an unpredictable meeting of minds. It's a fine way to spend an autumn afternoon.

Martin Lucas

An apple at Alballava.

dog coal

a nijuuin renga in autumn
Bowness-on-Solway, Hadrian's Wall
10 September, 2004

Participants
Denise Crellin
Alec Finlay (master)
Morven Gregor
Irene Leake
Martin Lucas (host)
Beth Rowson (co-ordinator)
Ann Ward

1 A probe landed on the planet Mars
  but failed to send back a signal.
2 Trekkies, fans of the cult science
  fiction series Star Trek.

First low light
the bee loud glade
is electric

    swallows peg the lines
    with chatter

word is out
that the Perseids
are to fall

    the saltmarsh sifts
    flecks of iron

from the chain gang
there comes a song
of hate

    lost in the sun
    baked mud cracks

startled by spray
the lizard
forgets its tail

    a curling bookmark
    in between chapters

on the *Mountains of the Moon*
giant heathers
living obelisks

    the goat herd steps
    over our sleeping bag

it's a job to know
whose feet are these
bundled in knots

    a catafalque
    from Port of Valletta

that night
the mourners broke
all the windows

    each frozen puddle
    invites another jump

dog coal
spits and crackles
on the hooky mat

    toast with its own
    black holes

the Mars Probe
signalling
nothing

    all the Trekkies
    pull their ears

mares' tails
still belong
in this world

    ... ... swish
    stand up to the Firth.

61

birdoswald fort

Approaching Birdoswald it begins to drizzle. Walking from car park to fort I get my first glimpse of the wall: grey, straight, solid and disappearing into mist eastwards. The bass riff from Floyd's *The Wall* pops into my head and my step adjusts to fit. The Renga Platform is already erected.

indoors
in anticipation
of a dreich day

The warmth of Douglas fir matches smiles from new-to-me-faces, I download the rucksack to the floor (not a hard drive in sight thank goodness).

The renga begins with introductions and green tea from an iron kettle. As six of us work on the *hokku*, Julie and Richard arrive in time to contribute to the selection discussion. The morning disappears as more links are added and, as the group begins to fuse, laughter punctuates the discussions more often. Taking a break for lunch, the weather deteriorates and we are all glad to be inside (well anticipated Alec!). We chat, eat and return to our own thoughts. Over smoked fish I become more aware of the exposed stone in the room – seemingly identical to that in the wall itself – and probably plundered for building work, centuries ago. Thus, we are really writing this renga from inside Hadrian's Wall. Yet another thought to add to the feelings and joy of writing it.

We resume; more links, more verses, more laughter, and more green tea: more than just a renga: a good day.

last stroll round the fort
the wind in old sycamores
screeching

David J. Platt

the walk back

a nijuuin renga in autumn
Birdoswald, Hadrian's Wall
12 September, 2004

Participants

Alec Finlay (master)
Morven Gregor
Irene Leake
David J. Platt (host)
Jacob Polley
Beth Rowson (co-ordinator)
Ruth Sheldon
Richard Thwaites

1 Aretha Franklin.
2 Spadeadam, site of the former blue streak missile launching test programme.
3 A carved phallus in the wall.
4 Ardbeg, a malt whisky from Islay.
5 Chough, a bird related to the crow.

Crenelated stone
catches and holds
the wind

    spate rushes shale beds
    further down the river

silken leaves
circle
in moon pools

    I climb home
    over patchwork hills

at every other stile
there's a new Aretha[1]
to sing

    a ram's horns
    blue heat

streaks from Spadeadam[2]
have seared
through the woods

    a carved cock[3]
    points west

I'm first up
so loud around the house
while you sleep

    losing a day
    on the pillow's a note

wax orders,
ghosts tumble over
the landlocked bridge

    paint it white
    no one thought to ask

shut the door
when you're through
the room shakes with firelight

    Ardbeg passed
    glass to glass

on the way back
the ice
meets itself

    boots crunch seaweed
    a chough glides into darkness

dawn breaks another
sleepless night
raw edged with toothache

    early daredevils
    paddle the surf

offered flowers
and orange peel
washed ashore

    shoeless
    into the distance.

album: from sea to sea

Lower Park, YSP.

1, 2 / camellia / fall

As part of my artist residency at Yorkshire Sculpture Park, 'Avant-garde English Landscape', I proposed a season of renga. The title for the series came from the magnificent camellias at Bretton Hall.

No-one has ever cracked together the platform quite as tightly as Nobby and Neil. It looked small in the spot we found for it, among tall beeches between Richard Serra's rocks and Sol LeWitt's grey brick plinths. One afternoon the sun was so fierce eight of us manhandled the plattie over the grass and beech masts into a patch of shade. For these renga days the smell of sun block was never far away.

I found my mastering tended more and more towards composite verses – there are three or four in some of the poems. Particular views from the platform influenced people's and this encouraged the combination of elements.

It's a fun and a funny thing to be sat on a deck of wood by a small stream, anchored on an English summer day in a park, observing and being observed. Grown-up visitors to YSP found as many ways as there can be to pretend us poets were invisible. Kids were openly curious. Our leisure and our labour interrogated the static monumental modernist sculptures between which people amble to and fro: material thingyness is all very well but, as Hamish Fulton says, an object cannot compete with an experience. A vote for the inner life then, for the memory map of renga.

(AF)

may in a vase

a nijuuin renga in spring
Yorkshire Sculpture Park, West Bretton
23 May, 2004

Participants
Lilli Brodner
Sheila Butterworth
David Fine
Alec Finlay (master)
Amy Gott
Morven Gregor
Alex Hodby (co-ordinator)
David Lewis
Gerry Loose (host)
Helen Lucy Pheby
Beth Rowson
Josie Walsh

1 Goose grass, *Galium aparine*, also known as sticky willy, cleavers or hayriff.

2 From the John Lee Hooker song.

Passed behind us
as we go
shared giggles, goose grass

    bracketed between parents
    three goslings

a family picnic
green fly
on the cups

    the girl yells
    I'm just pretending

over the hill
gently breathe
another mirage

    petroleum torches
    jets rumble on

scanning night sky
for the plough
taste of ginger

    consumed with a touch
    the stolen recipe

used over years
until perfected,
or cast aside

    house keys collect
    on her chain

she's fumbling
for the catch
in the moon

    lost in cataract eyes
    ripe for treatment

steamed windows
the jams cool
in jars

    thumping the piano wildly
    the cat runs

first frosts
mean retuning,
playing the blues

    to the end of the year
    boom! boom! boom! boom!

what was that?
what was that?
noticing the holes in my sock

    the first mushrooms
    with a little garlic

birthday breakfast
on a tray –
May in a vase

    the breeze whispers
    turn your face to the sun.

backwinter[1]

a nijuuin renga in summer
Yorkshire Sculpture House, West Bretton,
17 July, 2004

Participants

Anne Brook
Alec Finlay (master)
Alan Halsey (host)
Alex Hodby (co-ordinator)
Daphne Huberry
Jane Livingstone

1 Backwinter: Elizabethan expression
for a period of cold weather following
the first days of spring. 'A backwinter
or an after-winter is more raging,
tempestuous, and violent than the
beginning of winter' (Thomas Nashe,
Summer's Last Will and Testament).

2 The tori arches of Japanese temples
seen from a Bullet train.

3 Fly agaric mushrooms, *Amanita
muscaria*, famous for their
hallucinogenic powers.

Sheet lightning, thick air –
dark lines pressed
through the corn

  ragged clouds
  cross a petrol sky

the weekend begins
drinking tea at midday
with an empty head

  replete I follow my shadow
  on the long walk home

making clapping sounds
could we be
any closer to the fire

  another mitten turns up
  stuck behind a drawer

squashed flat
the fly that landed
between pages 8 and 9

  paper tear
  paper tear

with flour and water
she smoothes a landscape
for the Hornby double-o

  blurred red arches [2]
  glimpsed from Shinkansen

any moment now
we'll hear a snail
answer back

  leaves patter the earth
  draw our eyes higher

a silver fruit
the autumn woods
look past me

  fly agaric in their scarlet
  promise a happening

lizard-like
I catch the sun
scamper up the nearest tree

  zoom by the Ferrari
  are you mad?

the afternoon breeze
will be all
camellias remember

  slit backwinter light
  you wrap your robe

that christmas cactus
is still
in a right muddle

  tangled washing unfurls
  I lose my horizon.

dens and dares

a nijuuin renga in summer
Yorkshire Sculpture Park, West Bretton
7 August, 2004

Participants
Jack Ashton
Phil Bilzon
Vanessa Brown
Claire Cullingworth
Annie Eagleton
Alec Finlay (master)
Jackie Hardy (host)
Helen Lyle
Beth Rowson (co-ordinator)
Lynn Semour
River Wolton

1 This could be a wheelbarrow or
ancient burial mound.

Wade in the sea, arms raised
a rising band of cold
parts the afternoon

    diving in he fractures
    the shadow of the boat

gulls cut the sky –
Freya chases silver kisses
through spangled waves

    round bulbs blink, shutters down
    a final portion of chips and benches

gathered in quilts
stumbled in bed socks
thick stew on my mind

    driving home in the dark
    a spade clangs on the icy barrow

turning over the keys,
that grave was always
a little too well kept

    The *Lamb of God*
    rings round my ears

she leans closer
whispers, we can,
but we have to be quiet

    some thin music
    clipped from your tapes

half-way there
spiky palms
seen from above

    another metropolis
    FOR ALIENS ONLY

caught without papers
or pass
under a gallows moon

    trees stripped bare
    moths turn away

the bus south is on time
a crouched crow
thinks about it

    let's get out of here
    fingers fret at a scarf

count careful stitches
invent a life for the stranger
named on the label

    get changed for P. E. class –
    it's athletics on the fields

running from bright sun
a surprise of bluebells
in the beech wood

    dens and dares
    hiding the eggs.

wavy lines

a nijuuin renga in summer
Yorkshire Sculpture Park, West Bretton
4 September, 2004

Participants
Matthew Black
Alec Finlay, (master)
Andrea Freeman
Stuart Holt
Jane Livingstone
Marjorie Newlove
Helen Robinson (host)
Beth Rowson (co-ordinator)
Fred Schofield (host)
Kate Simpson
Andrew Wattie

Cupped poppies and apples
jelly set in jars,
the season sways

    first drops of rain
    on the kitchen window

two soaked cats
paw their whiskers
in the moon

    the boys' eyes close
    and flutter

at the allotment
the snowman's nose
an icy leek

    his dahlias
    caught by the frost

flags unfurl
diesel engines choke
to life

    under paper folds
    the consequences are . . .

a parallel walk,
a tug of grass,
entwined necks

    their fingers touch
    between the thorns

do the aliens
realise
we are praying?

    nuns play skipping games
    in the cloisters

a harvest
of black sloes
soon to be drunk

    wavy ploughed lines
    trees in rags

knackered pipes,
a bright bucket
in every room

    since the operation
    she can't manage stairs

wax on linen
rubs the image
of a knight

    lighter clothes now
    the sky a different blue

too small
for the camera's focus
the speedwell

    wellies in the porch
    after the ramble.

Vicky Hale, Gerry Loose, rengaistas on the woodland platform.

the woodland platform

You can still see the traces of the rusty tram lines in the paths that run through the hidden gardens at the old tramway on Glasgow's Southside. Beneath the raised beds there are concrete caves leached with heavy metals from the site's industrial past. Before the trams this place was an orchard, and now it has been transformed into a contemporary contemplative garden, with a lawn spread around a beautiful gingko tree and, farther off among the trees, an oak growing straight and tall through the middle of the woodland platform.

This is the first permanent renga platform. I dreamt of a house built around a tree, inspired by *The Parliament of The Birds*. Together with Chris Rankin of City Design, who composed the gardens, and my old friend David Connearn (a collaborator on the the original renga platform), we worked up a design in oak with four strong columns and an angled roof. Beneath the seats that define the house is a Xylotheque, a library of wooden books with samples of the native woodland.

People use the platform every day, to shelter from Glasgow's drizzle or on those rare days when a body needs some shade. And they use it for renga – in that green place what could be better than outdoor poetry?

(AF)

gloved in prickles

a nijuuin renga in summer
the hidden gardens, Glasgow
12 June, 2004

Participants
Laura Boyd (age 10)
Mirren Boyd (age 7)
Janette Brown
Karen Currie
Robbi Shaof Enge
Gerrie Fellows
Alec Finlay (host)
Simone Fleming (age 13)
Morven Gregor
Vicky Hale (co-ordinator)
Michael Hughes
Jo Kinnear
Gerry Loose (master)
Billy Love
Lorena Lozans
Rosie McNeill
Beth Rowson
Ranjana Thapalyal
Khushi Usmani

1 A shield bug climbed the oak's trunk
all day.

In the shallows
the heron fishing
through her own reflection

    clouds moving on birch bark
    fish scale in light

the moon
kissed by ripples
a broken teacup

    sky overrun by branches
    settle in stone

asleep but alive
all beings
still wait

    grey slush shushing
    the buses arriving

skinheads kiss,
paper news rolls on
my head is low

    gloved in prickles
    shaved tenderly

nor flower nor birth
moved by instinct
a cruel spine

    ouch!
    Damn Yankee Cactus

needles drop
head down into sand
sharp at both ends

    ants march home
    each with a grain of thought

left over
from harvest festival
tinned pear halves

    radio plays
    at half mast

space
limbo
if you can

    the scar
    turns darker

a thief
creeps deeper
into the night

    chubby elbows crouch down
    hands play pebbles

a beetle dives
off petalled silk
colours parachute below

    I'm a shield bug, who are you?
    which sign is green?

leave the window open

a nijuuin renga in summer
the hidden gardens, Glasgow
24 July, 2004

Participants
Irene Brown
Larry Butler
Ken Cockburn (master)
Mandy Haggith
Vicky Hale (co-ordinator)
Peter Manson (host)
Laurie Purvis
Angus Reid
Ruth Sheldon
Nuala Watt

Summer-camouflaged,
our little hilltop shelter
fortified by tea

    unseasonal rainfall
    each hello undiluted

a circle, a square,
grey scale measurement,
and one pair of sandals

    scatter of glad feet
    unlines the raked gravel

fireside dreams,
crackle of birch-twig bones
aching for ice cream

    happed figures
    curl on the frozen pond

brushes her hair,
telling a made-up story
which just keeps going

    red blots a page of his book,
    my pillow cleans the cut

chink of glasses
against the wet pavement
rain runs in torrents

    you can't resist,
    remove your shoes

runs after bees
try to catch some honey,
dry biscuits for lunch

    a wasp at last gasp
    passes on too-ripe fruit

candle wax drips
down the old bottle –
a withering turnip

    who hammered gold leaf
    across the green vault?

an escaped gift-giver
in the shape of a garden
hunted by no-one

    on her silvery wire she walks
    down the children's voices

draws the curtain on smells
from an orchard,
leave the window open

    with her eyes shut tight
    she hears the foetus grow

iris pokes out
an old pair of shoes
on Tuesday

    with full bladders we finish
    by soaking the compost heap.

feasting on mushrooms

a nijuuin renga in autumn
the hidden gardens, Glasgow
11 September, 2004

Participants
Norrie Bissell
Dominic Boyle
Richard Broadhurst
Irene Brown
Colin Clark
Ken Cockburn (master)
Anne-Marie Culhane (co-ordinator)
Lesley Stirton
Colin Will (host)

Wind shakes the trees
leaves hang on for now
the passing train

    slugs feast on toadstools
    but leave the children's wishes

sound asleep
a tiger's face
glows in the dark

    earth turns
    a worm wriggles

with silken moves
dancers merengue
through the night

    greenfly don't affect
    the taste of the beer

where he goes on holiday
determined
by his bottletop collection

    Cathkin Braes getting higher
    as vultures disgorge waste

from picking over
the bones of the past
we start afresh

    yes –
    but first brush your teeth

Saturday morning
weekend fathers
spend time with the kids

    at the theme park
    a moorhen nests on the volcano

see that hothouse
we can grow everything there
except maybe the moon

    freezer fruits
    brighten a baked rice pudding

listen to the howl
of thon wind
through the catflap

    learning the violin
    a solitary occupation

sound of the port city
heard by dolphins
through spinning propellors

    sunsets turn back towards Mull
    as the days lengthen

in celebration
the girl pins a sprig of rosemary
to her hair

    to get a better view a lamb
    stands on its mother's back.

twenty-four-hour hyakuin renga

A *hyakuin* is the great classical form of renga, used in such famous poems as Sogi's 'Three Poets at Minase' and 'Three Poets at Yuyama'. To match the renga masters of five hundred years ago is impossible, for we have neither the literary skill nor the cultural depth of allusion, but the more renga I experienced the more I became fascinated by the periodicity of each day, the rhythm of morning unfolding into afternoon. This led me to extend the renga day to its fullest measure and, on three occassions to date, a gang of poets have sat down together at noon and renga'd on through to bleary-eyed noon.

The first of these twenty-four-hour performances was hosted by BALTIC. The title defined the structure: '*four stations: work–rest–eat–sleep*'. Within the term of the hyakuin each poet takes his or her share mastering and they can rest and sleep when they wish – that said, few of us got more than two or three hours kip. What we gained by the close was the sweetest natural high.

The first *hyakuin* renga was blogged live on the BALTIC website and will soon be published on the renga platform website. The second was held in the jungly Camellia House at YSP on a freezing midsummer's night. Later that summer we completed a hyakuin under a clear starry night, sat out on the woodland platform at the hidden gardens.

Hyakuin brings people close – when three of you are sitting shivering at 3 a.m. and someone rustles out of their sleeping bag and tramps their way towards the platform you want to give them a big hug. All of us recommend it to anyone with a good sleeping bag and charcoal handwarmer.

The schema for each *hyakuin* was authored by an expert in renga. The thematic stepping stones led us in some interesting and occasionally rather odd directions but, when you're dog-tired and have been writing for eight hours non-stop, it can be a relief to have some clear instruction. I have included the schema here. We kept to a steady pace of four-and-a-half verses an hour.

(AF)

camellia house midsummer hyakuin renga

a hyakuin renga at Midsummer
The Camellia House, Yorkshire
Sculpture Park, West Bretton
noon–noon, 21-22 June, 2004

Nine poets
Paul Conneally
Anne-Marie Culhane
Alec Finlay
Linda France
Morven Gregor
Jackie Hardy
Alex Hodby
Gerry Loose
Beth Rowson

Renga schema: Jane Reichold
With thanks to Alex Hodby

1 Tir na nOg: Land of Youth in Irish myth.
2 High Possil, a place in Glasgow that Gerry Loose personifies as someone like the pontiff with a big hat.
3 Murasaki Shikibu, author of *The Tale of Genji*.
4 Captain Scott of the Antarctic.

The floor's a place
for an outdoor feast,
food in a basket

    a quick rub with a dock leaf
    and all is well

yesterday's moon
still shining in the bowl
of her throat

    upside down
    pores not gills

too large for the pond
the carp circling
only one way

    the shadows beneath
    her eyes grow darker

a tongue wags in with
in that dress
you'd expect nothing less

    the small boys pee a row
    of zeros in the snow

urged on
the vicar steps
off the church tower

    goosewing
    into the harbour

oiled
cormorant
can never be cleaned

    the shop assistant eyes up
    stains on his jacket

dark archipelagos
and outlined islands
where they may go

    the honeymoon, paid for
    by his parents

you're always beautiful
muttered
to the daisies

    they bury the lamb
    in the half–light

spring's broken,
she shakes the watch
against her ear

    another spaceship enters
    the orbit of the moon

radios crackle
as an electric storm
kicks in

    bake the pears whole
    in sugar and red wine

the burn is brackish
a race of rust
and shed wool

his beard unstuck
we recognise Santa Claus

lost in the woods
Hänsel and Gretel
could only eat gingerbread

growing up fast
she slams the door

in the face of it
the waiter rolls
the dragon's eyes

looking down
stairs can be dangerous

the elixir's made
of coltsfoot wrapped in
butterbur leaves

untie the ribbons
on the Maypole

making for the open
two hares chase
across the down

we stagger home
for the love of Bowmore

sandy toed
shoes on our heads
wading tidal flats

spun, spun, spun
into a waltzer kiss

a line of light
traced onto sky
my head aches

on the long flight east
two orange dawns

these fried peaches
are they breakfast
or last night's tea?

first win of the season
we follow the moon

cry of an owl
circling
whose hunting who?

in the dark
we almost felt the same

the differences
between our bodies
get less with age

despite the bleeps
we talk over everything

fuck this!
fuck that!
is all the walls say

    the new school
    ringed by a six foot fence

we catch flies
for the biology teacher's
flesh eating plants

    popcorn spills over
    at the late night double bill

wiping off
her make-up
on the last bus

    if you sit still long enough
    you can watch the flowers open

in the birthing pool
the baby slips out
from liquid to liquid

    my ears pop as we enter
    the channel tunnel

for the love of country
I fled
and now you send me back?

    a birthday present
    she keeps the receipt

locked in a drawer,
an amulet,
a loaded gun

    arms raised for St Jerome
    the blood bubbles

across the land
wells spring
spreading black poison

    nightshade
    cut with a scythe

the charcoal burners camp
in the middle
of Oak Wood

    a twist of smoke
    plies through the mist

at the crater's edge
disturbed by feet
a pebble dances down

    she fell in love
    with her psychoanalyst

together on a couch
a woman
and her cat

    fingers in a bowl
    of tormentil

a whole childhood
along ditches
of frogspawn

    my nose led by
    smells of wild garlic

walking to the souk
for lemons
and a heel of ginger

    the bitterness wears off
    as time goes by

an undertaker
practices his tuba
in the moonlight

    first hint of frost
    cracks the gardener's resolve

the whole street's washing
sooted up
by Mr. Smith's bonfire

    even the blue ribbon
    has turned to ashes

shouldn't it be gold
that is found
at the end of the rainbow?

    spiral notebooks and other
    tiny packaged objects

what can I say,
mice have been at the
snowdrop bulbs again

    up and up
    through the dead leaves

still sitting
the swan beaks
her massive nest

    from the bank cows watch
    a narrowboat pass

which is the river?
which is a canal?
and which the sea?

    we sail them all anyway
    in search of Tir na nOg[1]

the High Possil's hat[2]
could only
suit you

    what is he to think
    all those hearts on her sleeve?

Lady Murasaki[3]
elegantly dabs
a welling tear

    everyone wants to be
    a workie at breakfast

pull up the blinds
and the moon will shine
on buttered toast

    the train's delayed
    by the wrong sort of mist

under a beech
the sheep gather
in closed circles

    she clings to his back
    as they cross the river

you see turquoise
behind your eyes
when he touches like that

    the ice cap
    stops melting

Scott crossed out[4]
the word 'wife'
and wrote 'widow'

    the auctioneer's hammer
    comes down with a bang

fourteen cock pheasants
go rocketing
over the hedge

    in her buttonhole
    a speckled feather

up before dawn
to the meadows
mushrooming alone

    he breathes out,
    it's only the moon

willow leaves
float onto and under
the old bridge

    our log pile shifts
    a yowl from the vixen

the smudge of scarlet
through glass you know
is Japanese quince

    painting outdoors
    a delight of warmer days

it takes more time
to hide decorated eggs
in their small garden

    the Buddha's topknot
    lifts him to the light

helicopter blades
whirl incessantly
overhead

    poets shift
    closer to the ground.

renga schema

1.	summer	36.	autumn moon
2.	summer	37.	autumn
3.	autumn moon	38.	love
4.	autumn	39.	love
5.	autumn	40.	lamentations
6.	misc.	41.	lamentations
7.	winter	42.	misc.
8.	winter	43.	misc.
9.	travel	44.	misc.
10.	travel	45.	misc.
11.	lamentations	46.	misc.
12.	love	47.	travel
13.	love	48.	travel
14.	love	49.	love
15.	spring flowers	50.	love
16.	spring	51.	love
17.	spring	52.	religion
18.	autumn moon	53.	religion
19.	autumn	54.	autumn moon
20.	autumn	55.	autumn
21.	autumn	56.	autumn
22.	winter	57.	travel
23.	lamentations	58.	love
24.	lamentations	59.	love
25.	misc.	60.	spring flower
26.	misc.	61.	spring
27.	spring flowers	62.	spring
28.	spring	63.	travel
29.	spring love	64.	lamentations
30.	love	65.	autumn moon
31.	love	66.	autumn
32.	love	67.	autumn
33.	misc.	68.	lamentations
34.	travel	69.	lamentations
35.	autumn travel	70.	misc.

71. spring flower	86. winter
72. spring	87. winter
73. spring	88. misc.
74. travel	89. misc.
75. travel	90. misc.
76. travel	91. autumn
77. love	92. autumn moon
78. love	93. autumn
79. love	94. misc.
80. misc.	95. spring flower
81. autumn moon	96. spring
82. autumn travel	97. spring religion
83. autumn	98. spring religion
84. travel and love	99. misc.
85. love	100. misc.

Renga Schema: Jane Reichold
This hyakuin schema was devised following the pattern used by Sogi in his "Solo
Sequence of 1492" as presented in Steven D. Carter's *The Road to Komatsubara*.

the hidden gardens hyakuin renga

Where midsummer in a glass house was bitterly cold, come August in Glasgow we were fine to write under the stars. This was an especially magical renga. It is not possible to convey how moving it is to be sat there writing as the sun is setting, writing as the evening star peeps out, writing when a full moon rises through crack willow. The poem is a mnemonic.

As well as gathering old rengaistas from Edinburgh and Glasgow, it was delightful that a frail but doughty Dick Petit came all the way from Denmark. It seemed to relax the whole thing and make it a wee adventure that we were writing outdoors. I have a strong impression of how many fine verses Ken Cockburn and Colin Will offered, and how Peter Manson's poetic stamina never faltered.

(AF)

the hidden gardens hyakuin renga

a hyakuin renga in summer
(night of the full blue moon)
the hidden gardens, Glasgow
noon-noon, 31 July–1 August, 2004

Nine poets
Larry Butler
Ken Cockburn
David Connearn
Gerrie Fellows
Alec Finlay
Peter Manson
Dick Petit
Beth Rowson
Colin Will

Renga schema: Paul Conneally
With thanks to Anne-Marie Culhane,
Morven Gregor & Linda MacDonald

1 Quigong, system of exercises, rather
   like Tai Chi, for moving the Chi (Qui)
   around the body.
2 The Gaelic poets Meg Bateman and
   Sorley Maclean; the room was
   Sorley's room as a child on Raasay
   described in 'Hallaig'.
3 After Jacques Prevert, 'je suis la lampe
   qui me guide'.
4 Samphire, *Salicornia europaea*, a
   seaweed delicacy, treat & eat like
   asparagus.
5 Selkie, a Scottish folk name for a seal
   person.
6 Famous mountain pass in the
   Arrochar Alps.
7 Ted Hughes and Sylvia Plath.

Summer feet enter
hover at varying heights
above stone chippings

    the murmur of children
    building bird boxes

hearing aid feedback
cymbal sounds
go on and on

    the cat's and the dog's noses twitch
    reading each other's minds

a lunar eclipse
draws a russet curtain
on summer's plans

    viewing the apple orchard's
    transient constellations

why try so hard when
our words fall into silences
and so will the leaves?

    starting to speak at the same time
    eyes glance down

it doesn't matter
yet truly I did think
he would be interested

    a bouquet of crocuses
    on balance, a bad idea

so, a blue tree,
there in the top corner
en plein air au Barbizon

    Paris in springtime
    without loneliness

across the table
the children exchange
arguments and kisses

    there's a face you'd leave home for
    he says of the waitress

pulling her mink tighter
fur buttons too fat
for their holes

    bored by the long break in play
    they throw snowballs at the spectators

teeth gritted
then the song that gets everyone
up on the floor

    dazzled by the glitter ball
    over silent fields

a famished wasp
charges its ring tone
on the last bramble

    that water drop sparkling web
    invisible? anything but

ignoring the blind spot
and pulling out, the passenger's
right foot twitches

  smoke, wrote Brecht, *while you drive –*
  if it goes out, something's wrong

late summer
closing the door of her mother's house
for the last time

  a flat palm
  smashes open the garlic

angled lemons
outshine
the chopping board

  green tea and Quigong on the
  long haul prevent jet lag

in the quiet
the monk offers the traveller
a blow job

  after the ceremony
  there's nothing to do but eat

early potatoes
already sprouting
but there's lead in the soil

  salt'n'sauce? both hesitate
  unsure of the other's tastes

forgetting herself
a mother on day-release
cuts up her lover's meat

  after breakfast they send out
  for more oysters

whether with or without
our noticing
the sun's almost gone

  the night was made by Provost
  MacTavish and his good lady

boxes crammed
with bread, vegetables
and cans of mixed fruit salad

  floating amongst it all
  a big dollop of vanilla

the Lismore ferry –
vehicles, and fattened calves
heading for market

  stuff your bloody correctness
  you'll lick arse if you have to

sixteen shirts every week,
they don't iron themselves
you know

  flat white drifts
  crunched in footprints

dog shit melts
a hole
in fresh snow

his paintings emptied
till they were all sky

two stars
tell us the night is cleared
for darkness

some theorists forget
that thinking is a bodily function

he throws the beach ball higher
so she's forced
to stretch

the lines of labour
written on her belly

in the loft
the last train to Partick
runs all night

fumbling through his euros
at the Skye Bridge toll

at Sligachan we trace
the first and last of the snow
on Sgurr nan Gillean

Meg asks to see Sorley's room,[2]
the window that looked to the west

now the weather's warmer
she shortens her skirts
for Blythswood Square

after the demo paper every where –
another man's job

hosing down the corpses
pale human flesh –
Ché, Marat, Christ

I am the lamp
which guides me

even when you can't see
beyond your nose
follow the smell of smoke

lighting cigarettes in the rain
hunched together

the callgirl's nickname
for Henri Toulouse-Lautrec
was *Teapot*

reading the leaves
marriage, briefly

an out of tune piper
lamenting the dead
at the gates

marked PRIVATE
she can just see bluebells

Spring Bank Holiday
everyone hits the road
signposted SOLITUDE

    too many cooks
    spoil the pancake race

in the evening
nodding off on the sofa
startled by the phone

    father in Australia
    talks mostly of cricket

dew freezes the outback
radar is ranging
the moon

    commuter's day – leave before
    sunrise, return after dark

cast
catch nothing
cast

    The Waterfall of the Maiden
    icy in June

damp patches on her blouse
a mother's surprise
supply on demand

    we've come to expect
    food, fuel, gratified desire

the leaves come off
a glut of green
tomato chutney

    mulch under wellies
    kicked into the porch

the cats hope to impress us
with small overnight deaths
left on the mat

    from the oak a candle
    falls down and out

we've brought a night light
for the little one's
next visit

    leave the frogspawn alone
    you'll get all sticky

the tadpole succumbs
to a carp –
so much for evolution

    picking the samphire[4]
    at low tide

a selkie you say?[5]
already wondering
how she'll taste

    her past lovers lie
    heavily on his side of the bed

a torrid night
in the attic the moon
slips through the panes

    sweat up The Rest and Be Thankful,
    wish for a flat tyre

let down once too often –
from now on the failures
will be beheaded

    clear-cutting the rainforest
    the tribe gets whooping-cough

from under their shrouds
feet of men, feet of women,
feet of children

    at the school nativity
    the angel kicks the donkey

tempers rising
Ted slaps
Sylvia back

    even in the silly season
    poets don't make the headlines

you miss one week
and the recycling box
takes over the hallway

    pungent smoke from next door
    they say he saves the ash

shrivelled little figs
that never made it
to the table

    swirling a late cup of milky tea
    what she'd like is sunshine

wedding day breakfast
coffee with whisky
then whisky

    eggs over easy
    on rye

like sprinkled pepper,
these moles on your back,
or stars

    after weeks of deciding
    they named her Cassiopeia

now she sets ablaze
the horizon
of his eightieth year

    new clothes for Easter
    dancing in the street

all mouth this spring
lots of flounce
but nowt left hanging

    allotments flourish
    all the way to the summit.

the hidden gardens hyakuin renga

1. (hokku) summer
2. summer
3. NS
4. NS
5. autumn moon
6. autumn
7. autumn
8. NS
9. NS
10. spring (flowers)
11. spring
12. spring (love romantic)
13. love (NS, familial)
14. love (NS, lost)
15. winter (animal)
16. winter (sport)
17. NS (music)
18. autumn moon
19. autumn (fruit)
20. autumn (spider)
21. NS motor vehicle
22. NS literary allusion
23. summer (sadness, not love)
24. summer (flower/plant)
25. NS
26. NS (train/plane)
27. spring (religious)
28. spring (sense of wellbeing)
29. spring (flower/plant)
30. love (young)
31. love (kindness)
32. love (sexual)
33. NS (movies)
34. NS (class)
35. autumn (festival)

36. autumn moon
37. autumn (weather)
38. NS (politics)
39. NS (domestic chore)
40. winter (clothing)
41. winter (smell)
42. NS
43. NS
44. NS (bodily function)
45. summer (love)
46. love (NS)
47. love (hobby/pastime)
48. spring travel (Europe)
49. spring (mountain)
50. spring (long ago)
51. NS (crime)
52. NS (work)
53. religious figure
54. autumn moon
55. autumn (fog)
56. autumn (love)
57. love (artist featured)
58. love (sadness)
59. NS (Scotland)
60. spring (flower)
61. spring (crowds)
62. spring (kitchen)
63. NS (facial expression)
64. NS
65. winter moon
66. winter (travel)
67. summer by a river
68. summer holiday (Wales)
69. NS (baby)
70. NS

71. autumn (vegetable)
72. autumn (leaves)
73. autumn (animal)
74. NS (falling things)
75. NS (future)
76. spring (touch)
77. spring (death)
78. spring (delicacy/food)
79. love (romantic, NS)
80. love (jealousy, NS)
81. summer moon/love (sexual)
82. summer (bicycle)
83. NS (fairy/folk)
84. NS (lamentation)
85. winter (footwear/feet)
86. winter (festival)
87. NS (poet)
88. NS (scandal)
89. NS
90. autumn (bonfire)
91. autumn (sense of loss)
92. autumn moon
93. NS (taste)
94. NS (USA)
95. love (at first sight/first love)
96. love (for children)
97. love (in old age)
98. spring (upbeat)
99. spring (blossom)
100. spring (link back to the hokku)

Renga Schema: Paul Conneally
NS: Non-Seasonal verse

renga commentaries

On the renga platform we practise the arts of writing, reading, listening and sitting. (AF)

Resonance with space, time, place. In the moment, comes and goes, cannot be held. Something enters then departs, the rest of time is 'open waiting'. (AMC)

The content of a renga day is silence, words, time and experiences. (AF)

The act of writing renga is almost always more important as a piece of art than the finished renga itself. (PC)

The platform is an experience in itself – to be both in the open and to be in a defined space. (TR)

Our method is shared consciousness. (AF)

It was a day quite unlike any other creative process I have been involved in. The way in which the platform defined our space and held us together was reassuring ... The poem that snaked its way through the day became a reflection of all our thoughts – and I think this is why it is so satisfying to read, with levels of meaning that each verse alone couldn't convey. (AH)

I loved the way we inhabited the space. I really enjoy this principle of making art: intense, focused, collective, challenging – living, sleeping, breathing creativity. How can we do this again? (AMC)

Shared writing = shared mind. (AF)

I want to say what I have been saying to many people ... that the renga was the most engaging and pleasurable experience I have had with language + poetry + people for some time. My own practice is typically solitary, reserved ... and mediated. I cannot imagine any of these conditions ever changing. In fact, on the renga platform, living closely for a time with friends and strangers, they continued to apply. However, they did so in way that was explicitly negotiated and that brought these conditions out into an arena that was collaborative and social. (JC)

When someone who hasn't written this way before suddenly gets it, you see a smile spreading, like a flower opening up. (CW)

When actually experienced it opens up a whole host of synergetic possibilities. Everyone starts out nervous, sometimes trying too hard to be self-consciously poetic, or to fit into a preconceived mould of what Japanese poetry 'should be', but after a while people loosen up ...

and, as the event progresses, there seems to be a kind of meshing of the minds, as peoples' ideas start heading in the same directions. (AFi)

Life is like this, coming round the clock and every 90 degrees or less brings a formal requirement, a sense of time passing and appointments coming, and a few cocky words as we rush about, some jokes, some sighs, some signposts, some pointing off the road (though as a driver I hush distractions from passengers); sometimes the words come best when there's lots of distractions, don't know about when driving, though. (IL)

After the experience of renga I wrote these few words: *Si l'amour ne m'avait jamais été conte / j'inventrais des histoires / futilles et brèves / pour passer le temps.* (If nobody ever told me about love / I would be creating stories / light and short / to pass the time. (MM)

When a group dynamic gets going in renga there is the possibility that self-infatuation will subside. When this happens, consciousness is ready to take a leap – and bring us anywhere! Perhaps we should acknowledge the authors of a renga without attributing verses to individuals, not even giving their initials. In this way the ego, having nothing to anticipate, can dissolve. (GR)

By the end of our efforts on Saturday we were all practically in the centre of the renga platform looking expectantly at J as he selected the final two verses. And when we read over it again . . . there was a sense of, well, wonder: there were connections between verses in there that we'd never even consciously thought of. (AFi)

As a dancer who connects deeply with people through dancing with them (although I may not know their name, or anything else about them) I liked the fact that I didn't know most of the people at the start of the renga day, but got a curious, creative, sense of them through the lines they offered up as the day progressed and through simple interaction around the platform. Humans are often pretty raggedy and structure helps people to channel their creativity, their dreams, and generally express themselves more fully. (AN)

The renga was a strange experience because it was stripping away whatever I thought of as individual writing. Right at the beginning, when I thought that my offered verse continued the mood of an early morning train journey, but another verse was chosen, something more pastoral, –

then just when I thought, I cannot relate to these gentle verses, the verses were no longer gentle. Also, suddenly my verse was chosen, when I was least expecting it. Then it was inspiring. It is as if writing poetry is something completely different from what I thought it was. (JE)

If we look at the *hokku* as a pebble cast into a pool, the ripples will begin to manifest in the consciousness of the renga participants. At the end of the day there is an inkling that it is the one pool . . . (GR)

For me renga stanzas are very different to haiku – too often participants try to write haiku or haiku-like stanzas – I prefer natural sounding stanzas that can be read as phrases – no cut stanzas apart from in the hokku – the hokku being the only stanza that can be read as a stand alone haiku. (PC)

Distinct voices learning to harmonise respectfully. (LJ)

There's always a balance to be struck at these events, between privacy and participation. People approach to a safe distance, not understanding what is happening. More turn away than come closer, but they too are part of the poem. (CW)

It's my day as master, and I reflect on the role. You have to be sensitive to a developing theme; to be aware of pace and rhythm as the sequence grows; to know when a 'ground verse' is needed, and when a clever jolt will bring about a shift in mood or direction. With all that, you have to make sure everyone feels they are an integral part of the event. Then there's the time-keeping; sensing when people need just a little extra time to finish, while keeping track of the clock. You must be centred, and then it becomes easy. (CW)

A renga is relationship: the master and host poets are at the head of our day-long family. (AF)

My own creative energy ebbed and flowed – it's a pattern I'm used to, and I don't fight it. I enjoyed being able to present arguments from time to time and having the Master (and others) present counter-arguments to win the day. It felt very much like a team effort, and that feeling is important. (ML)

Eros gathers as the day passes: by the end of a renga there is a subtle charge of emotion, an elated buzz that arises immediately the poem is completed, then, a little death into exhaustion. (AF)

I'm starting to really feel when it works and when it doesn't for me, my creative body clock; this is really interesting, the highs and lows, it happens, it doesn't. Needing to move a lot, ideas stilled by sitting. walking and thinking – a walking renga? A slow walking renga. (AMC)

Putting the platform together we discover the importance of the correct order of things. We also discover how so much depends upon a found wheelbarrow. (CW)

At the bottom of the rucksack I pushed a black meditation cushion from Throssel Hole Priory. I like its size and I can sit comfortably for a few hours on it cross-legged. I put in two thick wool blankets, one for me and a spare tartan travel rug for someone else. Someone always needs a blanket as it can get pretty cold out there, sitting under the trees. I put in a flask of hot water, Russian Caravan tea and an old whiskey bottle with some milk in it. I carried an old white chipped enamel mug and a teaspoon. This was an indulgence and it meant that at some point, no matter what the conditions, I knew I could have at least one decent cup of tea in the day.

What I didn't take: I didn't take a pair of black fingerless gloves. These were passed to me silently on the platform and were perfect for writing outside and keeping warm. I did not take small charcoal hand-warmers. I would enjoy putting one of these beautiful blue velvet treasures down the back of my neck, where the heat seemed to radiate down through my whole body.

I did take my fountain pen and half a bottle of Waterman's black ink so that I could recharge my pen as and when. I tucked a quote from Grand Zen Master Riky into the front of my copy of the Renga Guidelines: 'in whatever one is doing, let it be done with a deep devotion of the heart'. I carried a Tibetan singing bowl and somewhere in my being I carried a reading from the I Ching, which asked for modesty and a low profile in all undertakings. Writing haiku outdoors on the renga platform means that I am in the elements and in the moment. I have no idea what the weather will do, who will come and join the group to write or whether I will be able to write anything myself. In a way the most important thing I carry is the knowledge that I have to be prepared to be unprepared. (JW)

Eat well afterwards. (AF)

They say that once you have written renku together you become cousins somehow – always linked. (PC)

Mastering a renga is probably one of the most exhilarating and tiring things I do – it requires total concentration whilst at the same time a kind of distancing from the personalities involved including one's own (PC)

During the renga I felt like a young apprentice, realising that to 'master' has so much to do with confidence and experience. My insecurities are put to rest when I think of the buddhist master paying tribute to his pupil for teaching him. Knowledge flows all ways. (AMC)

Everyone laughs = good verse. This is true not only for humorous links: there seems to be an immediate sense of relief and laughter when a verse is 'true'. Sometimes there is a group sigh. The wonderful thing is that these reactions arise naturally from the fidelity and freshness of the image, or the naturalness of the speech, not from wit or conceit. (AF)

For every master there is a master. (GL)

A renga is politics. The master poet is moderator of our little republic but just for one day. (AF)

I enjoyed 'listening in' and feeling what the group valued as a link-verse; the importance of shift; noticing a reluctance . . . as in most things in our culture, for stillness and quiet. (AMC)

Listen to each stanza offered as though it were your own. (PC)

All links are equal, though some appear more often than others. (DP)

Coming back to the renga now I feel that joy, that excitement again – the distance in time between last reading the piece now bringing me closer and finding new meanings in the links, new stories in the spaces between the stanzas. (PC)

Silence marks the internal borders of renga. (AF)

A renga is a reading as much as it is a writing. (AF)

Mishearings are common, and these release the unconscious: *incest* for *incense*, anybody? (AF)

I loved the way it was shown that bald statements have power: 'The bus south will go on time' etc. And the potency of the mundane: chips, benches, light bulbs etc. It made me reflect that the quotidian is the wallpaper of our thoughts and the soundtrack of our lives, so why not include it in a poem? (Annie)

I remember the invitation to the Renga . . . and I am glad to have made it. Is it a sacred ceremony? It touches our connection to the seasons and it touches the freedoms and sense of beauty we share in words. It is generous and inclusive and really quite intense. In that circumstance of shared place and time it does seem to be a sharing of pains and joys and as such maybe, or certainly, ceremonial. A very unusual experience. How to introduce a purpose, other than aesthetic exercising to the event? Or is the purpose it serves absolutely obvious anyway? I think the factor that makes for hesitancy as to whether to call it sacred is the fact that there is no external sacrament being administered to us, and the sacred thing must be inward instead, the unsure element of inspirational vision, ourselves as mediums, and while that is true (and in my view as guaranteed as an external sacrament) we are just not used to it, and to doing things that way. (AR)

I wrote so many verses in my head in the twelve hours following the twenty four hour renga. When I tried to sleep on Sunday morning on the train, and in the car, I couldn't. Verse after verse forming, being refined, dissolving. I was even speaking as though delivering verse, attentive to every word I was delivering into the world. (AMC)

We worked, we got tired, we rested briefly, we kept going and we made something. Poesis, poiesis. (JC)

Whose turn to make the tea? (Trad . . .)

Leaves scatter in a sudden gust, laughter chasing them on. Words gather into a pile of autumn. (CW)

the ship I'm in

Ira Lightman: Can I ask where you date your introduction to renga?

Alec Finlay: Young, young, young, and off the bookshelves. There were a pair of beautiful books Cid Corman had sent my Dad from Kyoto in the early 1960s, *Cool Gong* and *Cool Melon*, of haiku translations – traditional Japanese books, stitched-by-monks-and-with-horse-hair-spirals-of-reed-pulp-paper kind of thing, with Cid's excisions of words biroed in. Then there was a grander book, *The Monkey's Raincoat*, a classic renga by the Basho school. The poem in that book did not interest me nearly as much as Cid's haiku, not back then, for it was more dependent on allusion, and I couldn't get to grips with what was going on. But the idea of a form of poetry that was shared caught my attention: the between-people aspect, more than the words.

Ira: There's a love of reading, rather than headlong "I must express" in your approach. And a love of finding the right context to read – the best looking book or performance event to frame the word-event.

Alec: You have to remember how late I came to writing. I was a publisher first and foremost, for ten years. Some time passed, as they say, and I fell back in love with haiku, gathering together the anthology of Scottish haiku and short poems, *Atoms of Delight*. But none of these literary activities led me to renga. That departure, or arrival, came when I uncovered an art practice of my own. An important urge was the desire to experience shared consciousness that renga proposed.

Ira: The words are put together with some of the craftsmanship of the builder in wood. There's a Tom Stoppard speech in a play of his, about the well-written line being springy like a dance floor or a cricket bat . . .

Alec: What I always remember is that at the first renga platform event (2001), after I had done the preamble explaining about what the day would involve; after everything was set up and the tea was made; after everyone was settled down; after the first verse was written; well, there was nothing left for me to do but take my own place and join in as a poet in my own right. It sounds ludicrous, but in a sense I had finally 'tricked' myself into writing. So, I sat down and began. How did you find it when you bumped into your first renga?

Ira: I turned up to the BALTIC, on the day you'd said. I was directed to your studio looking out onto the river. There was a group of people, with no particular airs, that felt like a group you'd walk into for a meditation class, or yoga class, willing, polite. And you were all sitting around the renga platform, which was a little like a Tardis console in shape, in my mind. There were lots of cushions. Tea served, from a metal pot. Concentration, as a noticeable group on a class day-out in the park on a very ornate public bench designed as a piece of public art by a modernist/socialist sculptor. I think I was ten minutes late, so you'd all started, and I roughly knew it was a poem that we all added to, decided a verse, and then all took off from that verse. I was given a pad, and started drafting my suggestion for the next verse. I knew we had ten minutes to come up with one, and then we'd all present what (if anything) we'd come up with.

Alec: Sounds like we were at the same thing. People often talk about the calm of that studio, and the homeliness, which I realise is something I give to it – I recognise the atmosphere from many comments, though it wasn't always a calm space for me, being my place of work, and being in an institution that had a strong imaginal gravity. I did enjoy those days, so like family picnics, as a way to bring a gentleness to the space, and share it with people, to a purpose. Something Wittgenstein says comes into this: *a beautiful light is shed by work.*

Renga is also close to that Cagean desire to find a mode of art that is identical with a mode of life (or a weather system, a natural operation). It has a concern with the politics of social relationships. Renga reveals and also moderates power relationships. It has a rule which says: listen to everyone. Counterbalancing that, it has a form of governance, the master – which is something that Cage worked against, but also embodies.

I asked the Irish poet Gabriel Rosenstock if he could – in some utopian world – choose between poetry and renga, between writing as a mode of sharing or writing as a solipsistic flexing of the consciousness muscle and he chose renga. We were exaggerating, of course. The point is that renga is a counterbalance to the social disaster that literature is.

Ira: Can I take myself back through some of what I see going on during a Renga day? I see everyone trying to write haiku – well, a two or three line imagist poem – I see that there are at least four constraints (that can be liberating): (i) don't repeat too much of either the theme or vocabulary of the previous verses, (ii) link, so that you don't repeat or drone (see i), and be sure to turn (but don't twist your ankle), (iii) keep within the season or theme, if there is one specified for that verse, and (iv) write a good renga verse. I see the role of the master poet to remind everyone of these rules or conventions, but only after at least one participant has gone wrong. In other words, they have repeated, gone for the wrong season, and so on. The master may say, you're nearly there, if it was only . . . and suggests a correction. We don't go back though: we all listen and learn as 'mistakes' happen.

Alec: Yes, the pedagogy is done within the process, but it mustn't detain you. There is no reason to say, if only you had written a verse more like X or Y. Each person learns from listening to how one verse follows and alters another; they begin to see the choices that are involved –

Ira: – Because there is, in a sense, so much to write. It is not a workshop in making small imagist poems – we do not have time to analyse each specific verse, and I can see that it isn't even useful to do so, for we need to write the next link. The more one does renga, the more one saves up a line, for the next time one does a renga. This used to be lines one might have worked up, and overworked, for a longer solo poem. I wonder if others learn to do this, to stop overwriting lines that are only good for renga.

Alec: During a renga day itself, ocassionally an unused verse will be recalled late on, perhaps when things are stuck and people are labouring. On these rare occasions, it feels as if one's consciousness had made a loop back through the comet's tail, picking up the grains of a word or image that can work. It's always fun but it won't work as a strategy – for the act of the mind gripping on to an image will prevent one turning a new link. The more you do it the more you enjoy how the poem is self-defining at each moment.

Ira: I guess I am drawing attention to why the renga space is like one's own writing space – writing by oneself for others. Isn't one of the origins of the Japanese tradition that the master is a very, very good poet and everyone

comes along in a sort of "masterclass", like a classical music class, where the
learner plays and the teacher says "now, see how I do it".

Alec: In Basho's case many of the poets in his school were very gifted in their own right. Also in classical Japan so many people knew how to write a haiku. It was the mark of being a civilised person. With beginners, every now and then they will say something so directly, so truthfully, and this is a release for the poem and everyone there.

Ira: Yeah, and many's the professional who cannot write a simple line and
needs the simple verses to offer clever links between. And can dazzle the beginner
at the rule of "don't repeat what's gone before" by technical analysis skills.

Alec: Sure thing. Like the German guy who was walking round the botanical gardens in Edinburgh when we had an outdoor renga platform event, and stayed for one link, not even long enough to sit down, and dropped in.

the wood stack settles, creaks
it will hold

Ira: I think one can love renga without knowing anything about renga or
the renga platform. It could survive on papyrus, like a fragment, when nothing
is left of our civilisation, and suggest a complex background you could guess
at . . .

Alec: In other words, a study of shared consciousness.

Extract from a *Conversation on Renga*, the complete text is available online at www.alecfinlay.com

index of renga 2001–2005

GREEN BANANAS
the hidden gardens, Gateshead (UK)

GROWTH WAITS FOR ITS MOMENT
Cockermouth (UK)

HADRIAN'S GHOST (S)
Hadrian's Wall (UK)

IN THE SIXTEEN HOUR NIGHT (V)
BALTIC, Gateshead (UK)

LEAVE THE WINDOW OPEN (S)
the hidden gardens, Glasgow (UK)

MAY IN A VASE (S)
Yorkshire Sculpture Park, West Bretton
(UK)

MURMUR OF BEES
Royal Botanic Garden Edinburgh (UK)

NO COAT
Edinburgh International Book Festival
(UK)

PERHAPS THE THRUSH (W)
the hidden gardens, Glasgow (UK)

PSYCHO–GEOGRAPHY
BALTIC, Gateshead (UK)

PURPLE INTO BLACK
Rothko Chapel, Houston (USA)

RENT WEB (S)
BALTIC, Gateshead (UK)

ROMAN HOLIDAY (S)
Hadrian's Wall (UK)

SECOND SUNDAY BEFORE
CHRISTMAS
Scottish National Portrait Gallery (UK)

SEMANTICS OF LOVE ON A ROCK
Green Mountain (USA)

SUMMER HATS
BALTIC, Gateshead (UK)

TALKING ON THE LAWN (S)
Hadrian's Wall (UK)

THE BLIND DOG
Swaledale Festival (UK)

THE FAMILY KNOT (S)
BALTIC, Gateshead (UK)

THE HIDDEN GARDENS HYAKUIN
RENGA (S)
the hidden gardens, Glasgow (UK)

THE HIGH ROAD
Scottish Poetry Library, Edinburgh (UK)

THE INDIAN TRAIL
the hidden gardens, Glasgow (UK)

THE LITTLE COLTSFOOT (V, W)
Royal Botanic Garden Edinburgh (UK)

THE RIVER RUNS BACKWARDS (S)
Hadrian's Wall (UK)

THE WALK BACK (S)
Hadrian's Wall (UK)

THORNS INTO BUDS
BALTIC, Gateshead (UK)

TIGHT AIR
Galway Arts Centre (Eire)

UNDER TALL TREES (V, W)
Dawyck Botanic Garden (UK)

UPRIVER (V, W)
Art.tm, Inverness (UK)

VAGUE RADIO (V, W)
Royal Botanic Garden, Edinburgh (UK)

WALKING BACKWARDS (S)
Swaledale Festival (UK)

WATCHING THE RAIN (W)
Royal Botanic Garden Edinburgh (UK)

WAVY LINES (S)
Yorkshire Sculpture Park, West Bretton
(UK)

WORST OF ALL ARE THE DWARVES (S
Olomouc (Czech Republic)

WRITING IN THE DARK (S)
BALTIC, Gateshead (UK)

NOTE
(V) published in *Verse Chain*
(S) published in *Shared Writing*
(W) published on the renga platform
website, www.renga-platform.co.uk
(Wl) published at:
www.balticmill.com/4stations/renga.php

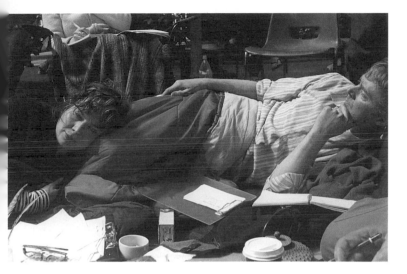

acknowledgements

I would like to thank all of the renga masters, especially Ken Cockburn and Gerry Loose; Morven Gregor, for her photography; and Anne-Marie Culhane, for her dancing.

I also extend my thanks to all of the venues and hosts, especially Alex Hodby, Sune Nordgren, Emma Thomas, Jude Watt, Judy Thomas, Mireille Martel, Miles Thurlow, Elliot Young, Ian Gonczarow, Andy Hodson, Helen Pheby, Nobby (Iain) Stephenson, Tom Trevor, Colin Will, Gavin Morrison, Fraser Stables, Phillip Parr, Michael Dempsey, Angus Farquhar, Linda MacDonald, Faith Liddell, Kevin Henderson, Robyn Marsack, Mathew Sweney and Steve Chettle.

I would also like to thank the following people for their help and support on the renga road: Beth Rowson, Jo Salter, David Connearn, Nina Sverdvik, Guy Moreton, Gabriel Rosenstock, Martin Lucas, Paul Conneally, Jane Reichold, Gavin Wade, Tito, new media bureau, electronicartist, Chris Rankine, Ed King, Ira Lightman, Cluny Sheeler and Lucy Richards.

Alec Finlay

small press series

Irish (2)
artist collaboration by Alec Finlay, Guy Moreton, Zoë Irvine & Tim
Robinson, et al, translations of 'Irisch' by Paul Celan. With an audio-CD
2002 ISBN 0-9527669-5-7 £10.00

Football Moon
football haiku by Alec Finlay
2002 ISBN 0-957669-4-9 £10.00

Cowboy Story
artist collaboration by Richard Tuttle, Heather Deedman, Zoë Irvine
& Alec Finlay
2002 ISBN 0-9527669-3-0 £10.00

Verse Chain: Sharing Haiku & Renga
guidelines, reflections and photographs on renga by Alec Finlay
& Martin Lucas, et al
2003 ISBN 1 0-904477-01-1 £10.00

Wind Blown Cloud
artist anthology of photographs collected by Alec Finlay
2003 ISBN 0-1-904477-03-8 £10.00

Friday 8 May
artist book by Alexander & Susan Maris; 13 original photographs by
Richard Demarco of Joseph Beuys in Scotland, with re-photographs
by the Maris
2002 ISBN 0-1-904477-04-6 £10.00

Bynames
artist anthology of invented names for real people collected by Epic Filly
2003 ISBN 0-904477-05-4 £10.00

Rosengarten
artist collaboration by Janice Galloway & Anne Bevan
2004 ISBN 0-9546831-0-2 £10.00

Turning Toward Living
artist anthology of circle poems, collected by Alec Finlay
2004 ISBN 0-9546831-1-0 £10.00

Mesostic herbarium
artist anthology of mesostic poems on flora, collected by Alec Finlay
With a CD-Rom.
2004 ISBN 0-9546831-2-9 £10.00 (incl. VAT)

The Book of Questions
artist anthology of children's questions, collected by Alec Finlay
2004 ISBN 0-9546831-3-7 £10.00

Shared Writing: Renga Days
guide to renga days by Alec Finlay, et al
2005 ISBN 0-9546831-4-5 £10.00

Also available: **Ideas Leave Objects Standing**
selection of recent works byDavid Bellingham
2005 ISBN 0-9546831-5-3 £15.00

All books are available from:

Platform Projects, 21a West Mayfield, Edinburgh, EH9 1TQ
www.platformprojects.org
info@platformprojects.org

Morning Star, Off Quay Building,
Foundry Lane, Byker, Newcastle, NE6 1LH
www.alecfinlay.com
alecfinlay@yahoo.com

YSP is an independent art gallery, registered museum and charity.
Registered charity number 1067908. YSP receives funding from:
Arts Council England, Wakefield MDC, The Henry Moore Foundation,
West Yorkshire Grants (a joint committee of Bradford, Calderdale, Kirklees
Leeds and Wakefield Councils).

Writing on the Wall is part of Hadrian's Wall Tourism Partnership's
Enrichment and Enterprise Scheme, a five year initiative funded by
One Northeast and other partners. Hadrian's Wall Tourism Partnership
is a public and private sector partnership developing sustainable Arts,
Business, Education, Tourism and Transport around the Hadrian's Wall
World Heritage Site. Writing on the Wall is an ARTS UK originated project
which it is delivering on behalf of the Partnership by working closely
with other public, private, voluntary and independent agencies in a series
of community based residencies and workshops.

A Calendar of forthcoming Renga Days can be viewed on
www.renga-platform.co.uk

The renga platform is in residence at Dharmavastu for the duration of 2005.
All enquiries about hiring the renga platform should be directed to
alecfinlay@yahoo.com

The publishers acknowledge support from the Scottish Arts Council toward
the publication of this title. The artist would like to thank BALTIC Centre
for Contemporary Art for supporting the development of the project and for
contributing to this publication.